KT-394-990

Absolutely

JOANNA LUMLEY

MPH
DAYTONA

Absolutely

JOANNA LUMLEY

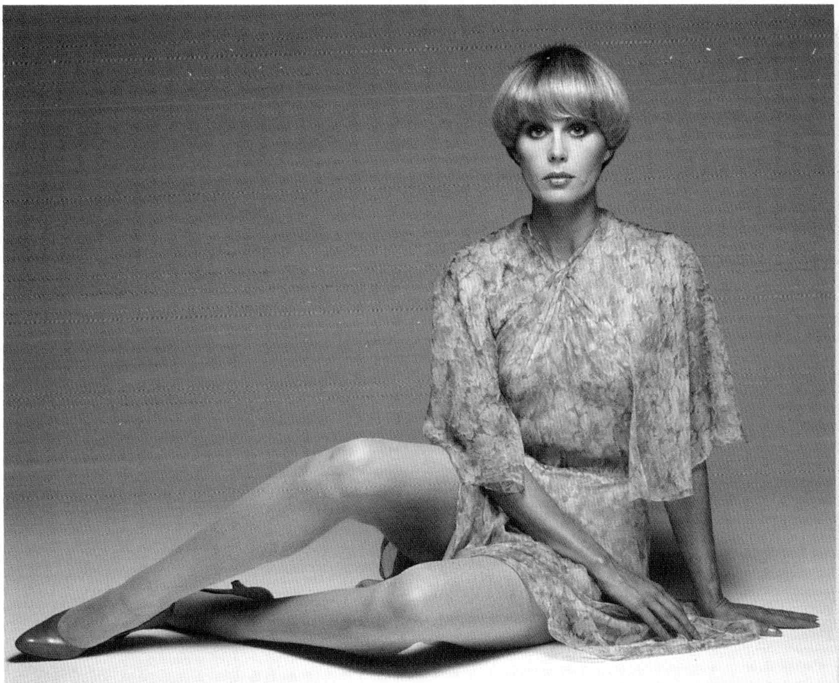

WEIDENFELD & NICOLSON

LEICESTER LIBRARIES

HA

Askews & Holts	19-Oct-2011
	£20.00

Contents

MATCH
Le crash
LA NUIT DE L'HORREUR
LEURS PHOTOS EXCLUSIVES

Half title: *Aged twenty in trendy grandpa vest. Lower eyelashes drawn on heavily. Trying to make my shoulders look narrower.*

Title page left: *In a Zandra Rhodes dress on Patrick Lichfield's motorbike. Rather shiny tights make the legs look like sausages.*

Title page right: *As Purdey in the* New Avengers. *An early publicity shot with the Purdey haircut unveiled.*

Left: *With Eric and Ernie when I appeared in their show. The theme was The Twenties and I had to sing 'Thoroughly Modern Millie.'*

Above: *Patsy's dreadful circulation meant that she was freezing cold even in the South of France and had to resort to rugs and magazines to keep the blood travelling round her raddled body.*

Introduction

I have hoarded things all my life; letters and lamp-stands, pencils and chairs, bales of cloth and used wrapping paper. I can't help it and I can't stop. I have in some way hoarded my very life, as there is in every room of our hugely overcrowded house something from long ago which reminds me of being a child or a lumpy teenager, or even a time before I was born when my parents and grandparents travelled with their regiments or duties around the Far East, Tibet and India. This amassing of memories serves me well, yet slows me down; nothing can be discarded without a 'chance to see again', as the BBC would put it, a repeat performance of its original role, yellowed and cracked now with time but bringing into sharp focus days and words and clothes from another age.

'You don't have to be posh to be privileged.' In an advertising campaign for Privilege Insurance that was my catchline: here I am dressed up as royalty for a portrait, hanging in a transport caff, which came alive and spoke these words to astonished customers.

However, nothing comes close to the power of photographs in evoking memories. My mother Beatrice, from whom I have inherited the hoarding bug (although mine is much more diluted than hers: she could actually feel sorry for a spoon or 'give a kind home' to a three-legged table) saved everything; pieces of string, abandoned lids, my sister's drawings and every magazine or newspaper she could lay hands on in which I appeared as a model. These she kept in old suitcases, dangling with labels saying 'Not Wanted On Voyage' or 'Barclay's Bank Nairobi' or 'Singapore'. Mixed with these relics of the time, when fashionable Britain was in the grip of mini-skirts and wigs, were letters and postcards from days before the days I could remember: and albums, envelopes and files of photographs. When these were added to the really colossal amount of press cuttings, publicity stills, reviews, old school reports and articles which I had amassed through the years, now cunningly concealed in bland-looking boxes and folders and trunks, it would be fair to say that it was an awe-inspiring collection.

Far from making it easier to have such a treasure trove to dig into to prepare this book, it has made it fifty times harder. For some reason

I want to show you, dear reader, everything I have: like an exhibitionist, or, to be frank, like a crashing bore, I want to say 'Oh look at this! We were on location in Canada' or 'Do you see that hat? I made it myself from a lampshade'. As my life stretches away behind me I find that I can still see the end of the tail as it winds back through films and campaigns, modelling trips and school plays, lost front teeth and my own baby boy. So the hardest bit has been what to choose and what to let drift; what might ring a bell in your own memory and what is honestly only there because I thought I looked nice in that dress.

Playing Desdemona with Michael Levete as Othello for the Old Harrovian Players. The costumes were on loan from the Royal Shakespeare Company. The character in front of the curtains is Richard Curtis, yet to leave school and begin his exciting and extraordinary career. Comic Relief was not yet born.

I have hoarded up memories too: to recall the names of girls in my class at school, of make-up artists and directors, I put my brain into slow-trawl and usually I come up with an identity. But memory can play fearful tricks, and I am stunned to find that I cannot remember the dates of any work I did after *Sapphire and Steel*. Perhaps my brain was marooned along with those valiant space travellers in an abandoned petrol station, slowly circling the cosmos, Sapphire in her blue dress and Steel still inhabiting the handsome form of the erstwhile Illya Kuryakin; for as actors we are all replaceable, memorable for a while if we are lucky, then fading to black as the world spins towards another goal. How I hate forgetting the people I have been so close to; in our world we are like a travelling circus troupe, trapeze artists, wholly reliant on each other, moving on from town to town, smiling and striking a pose even when there are only three men and a dog in the audience, packing our shabby cases in our tiny, dirty changing rooms, and moving on, moving on. Since I have played Broadway her old showbiz tunes rattle round my head more often, and 42nd street is a reality now, where there's no business like show business and plays open and shut like a butterfly's wings. We are guaranteed nothing, and that is the reason I chased after the caravans as they rumbled out of town; nothing is certain and every day is new. I find that rather thrilling.

Each picture I have chosen brings with it, like a gauze cloak, its own insistent story. Even a knitting pattern photograph has its own dignity (or actually its own sweat-inducing reality of how things were in 1965). My life has been long and eventful: sometimes, like the character Zelig from the Woody Allen film, I seem to have appeared everywhere and in everything. The far-away childhood and the 'Angela Brazil' boarding schools lead on to becoming a model in the sixties, and a Bond girl: after that, an Avenging partner of John Steed and a victim of Dracula give way to Hedda Gabler and Oscar Wilde; and behind all this are the travel documentaries and journeys and family and friends, besides crashing about as Patsy in *Absolutely Fabulous*. How on earth can I cram all this into one book? Well, I think I have made a pretty good stab at it, and I have included everything that is important to me that I think will interest you. Although I have never been the subject of the programme *This Is Your Life* I have been a guest on the show many times: and it seems that This Is MY Life, specially prepared for you, but in a luxury edition, containing everything but nuts.

To get off to a flying start I want to begin before I was born, to explain a bit about where I come from and why I was there. I want you to be interested, charmed, amazed and amused. This book is for you.

Out of India

More than a hundred elephants and their mahouts. You can tell which region the men are from by the way they tie their turbans. Each area has a slightly different look. This photograph taken out of my paternal grandfather's album makes me think it may have been from the great Durbar of 1908, a few years before the famous Delhi Durbar.

'Durbar' means festivity/celebration/huge event. Long ago it was commonplace for elephants to be used rather in the same way as horses were in the west, as beasts of burden and haulage and panoply.

My mother's family, the Weirs.

In the days of the British Empire it was normal for people to be born in a distant land, to live, work and be married abroad and yet to think of Britain as 'home'. Home was where you went on leave, by ship, staying for about six months before returning to India, or the Far East or Africa, or to what were called the colonies. On both sides of my family India was home for several generations. They were all soldiers at some stage, but their principal employment was in the political or medical services. Today it is hard to imagine the way people travelled in those days: by slow and unreliable motorcars on bumpy roads, in horse-drawn carriages and

My great–grandfather was known in the family as GrandPat: his name was Colonel Patrick Weir of the Indian Medical Service: here he is seen in his dashing white uniform somewhere in the Central Provinces of India.

His son Leslie was my grandfather. He was born in Ghazipur in 1883 and joined the 5th Cavalry of the Indian army. He laid out a nine-hole golf course in Tibet, sent seeds from rare Himalayan plants to King George V and spoke twelve languages.

steam trains, on horseback or on foot, on board ships with spartan accommodation; and yet the journeys were made, the post got through and telegrams remained the most reliable way of sending urgent messages. To travel home took weeks, not hours. Most children used to be sent to England to be educated, and often didn't see their parents for three or four years. Husbands and wives got used to being apart for months at a time. It was a different world.

My mother's father, Leslie Weir, was a diplomat; his naturally friendly nature made him a trustworthy and welcome guest in countries that were suspicious of the outside world, countries like Tibet and Bhutan. As he always took the trouble to learn the language and know the local customs he was able to remain on the friendliest terms with everyone he met, from kings and prime ministers to porters and grooms. My mother's mother Thyra was Danish but had been born in New Zealand, where her father Christian Sommers had set up his life and family in the 19th century. She met Leslie while she was in Burma; my great-uncle Bart, her brother, was building a hospital there, and because he was a bachelor at the time Thyra went with him to run his household. My grandparents' wedding was quite small and without the usual complement of family guests and close friends, as Burma was a long way from India and New Zealand.

Granny Weir, Thyra Letitia Alexandra Sommers as she was before she married, was an actress through and through, although she only appeared in amateur dramatics in India.

When my grandparents married in Rangoon Hugh Gaitskell was one of their pageboys, the one sitting at Granny's feet. Her brother Bartholomew is standing behind her, with a balding head: he had been building a hospital in Burma and Thyra went to keep house for him.

Granny standing at the right with her riding crop over her shoulder appears to be instructing the unknown photographer as to the best angle. In the distance are some of the horses which the men had ridden to reach the picnic spot. The women would have come up in open horse-drawn carriages (although my mother used to tuck her skirt into trousers which she wore under her dress and ride astride to parties and picnics like this one).

I wish I could remember Grandpa: I did know him when I was tiny, and I sat on his lap when he visited us in Hong Kong, but I only have a small blurry photograph of that occasion. Everyone loved him; he died, too young, of leukaemia and is buried in Kenya which is where my grandparents went to live when he retired; 'home' wasn't

England to them as they had never lived there. My grandmother Thyra had a dashing personality, great artistic talent (and temperament) and immense personal charm. Theirs was a life of duty, travel and recreation. Duty led them to Persia and Sikkim, Bhutan, Kashmir and Tibet and all over India and the Middle East. My grandfather was what was called a Resident, a sort of mix of an ambassador, advisor and go-between. Often the places he visited or resided were off the beaten track, and British India was keen to know how things were in these distant outposts; whether the ruler was sympathetic to the British or to Russia, the other super-power looming in the north, or the Chinese in the east, always ready to move in to what they saw as their own recalcitrant territories. He gathered and gave information, made friends, officiated at functions, and often collected seeds of rare plants to send back to His Majesty King George V and to Kew Gardens. Grandpa and Granny Weir lived in Residencies, quite grand buildings that came with the job; theirs was an Edwardian lifestyle, with hard work interspersed with dinner parties and point-to-points, hunting, shooting and fishing, tennis and amateur dramatics.

They had two daughters: Joan Mary, a tall blonde blue-eyed beauty, crack shot, artist and breaker of hearts, and then, seven years later, my mother Beatrice, black haired and green-eyed, a brave and kind-hearted tomboy. Both were sent back to be schooled in England, and for the girls, being seven years apart in age, these were solitary sojourns. They were looked after in turn by kindly but ancient guardians and they communicated with their parents by letter, as no-one telephoned in those days, least of all schoolchildren. In faraway Himalayan countries there was no electricity, let alone telephones. When my aunt left school she returned to India to be with her parents, just as my mother was being sent off to be a boarder in a cold country unknown to her, where she was not allowed to see other children in the holidays. She made her guardians' animals her friends, and from her I have inherited my love for all creatures great and small. Being at school she missed the great journeys her family made: my aunt Joan Mary used to send her drawings and descriptions of the extraordinary and exciting places they visited, notably Tibet and Bhutan. My mother, at school in Hampshire, would think of the pony she had left behind in Sikkim, and imagine their long trips on horse and foot with mules and yaks; and she would dream in Urdu, her first language, taught to her by her *ayah*, her Indian nursemaid. As soon as she left school she went back to rejoin her family in the great sub-continent she considered her home all her life.

Thyra cutting a dash on a hot day. Even in heat-waves or monsoons you were expected to dress properly, with petticoats and stockings, hat, gloves, and in this case a parasol.

POTALA
LHASA.
BEST WISHES FROM
LIEUT.-COLONEL AND MRS. LESLIE WEIR.
THE RESIDENCY,
GANGTOK, SIKKIM.

My grandparents' Christmas card. The Potala in Lhasa was the palace of successive Dalai Lamas before Tibet was invaded by the Chinese. In the 1930s Grandpa had become a close personal friend of the thirteenth Dalai Lama, the spiritual and political leader of Tibet; Granny was the first European woman to visit this majestic and secretive capital city.

Things haven't changed much; anywhere in the world this sort of formal photograph is familiar to this day. Carpets were often spread on the grass, making any lawn or courtyard into a grand outdoor salon. Granny always took her dogs with her on these long diplomatic journeys.

My father's family, the Lumleys.

My father, James Rutherford Lumley, was born in Lahore: his father, Charles Chester Lumley, was the son of a clergyman, William Faithfull Lumley, the chaplain of Chelmsford Prison; the family was large and money was fairly scarce. His great-grandfather was the splendidly named Adjutant-General to the Indian Army in 1798, Major-General Sir James Rutherford Lumley, and even though young Charles was brought up in England he decided to follow his ancestors to India to seek his fortune. I don't think it was a fortune, but it was a respectable and responsible job, running a big bank in western India, as it was before the creation of Pakistan. He met and married my grandmother, Ella Marion Young, in India and like my mother my father was sent home to school, seeing his parents only once in four years. He had three sisters, Rosa, Arabella and Isobel; when my grandfather retired from the bank the whole family left to live in England, but my father was to return to serve in the Indian Army as a Gurkha officer.

As I get older there are a thousand things I wish I had asked my parents. I never met my grandfather Charles: nor for that matter did my mother, as he died before she and my father met. I wonder what kind of a man he was: my aunts said he was a very gentle man, mild-mannered and humorous. I hardly knew my grandmother Ella either, but I have the beautiful little diamond necklace she wore on her wedding day; it was left to me by my aunt and I shall leave it in turn to the next generation. My latest resolution is to write who, when and where on the back of every photograph I have. It may take ages but as my own memory fades (not yet! but surely soon) it is the least I can do for my grandchildren. You think you will never forget an event, or that someone's face is too familiar or well-known to need identifying but I shall do it just in case. Memory is like smoke. You can see it clearly...and then it is gone, leaving not a trace behind.

My grandfather sits in the centre with the staff of the Bank of Bengal in Lahore. This must have been a day of celebration as they are wearing garlands of flowers; the blooms look like tuberoses and marigolds, maybe carnations. I love the custom of garlanding: men look extra-manly when decked out in blossom.

The status of Viceroy of India was sometimes considered to be even higher than the King's; the stupendous pageants and awe-inspiring ceremony that attended his every move were a feast for the eyes. Here in a photograph taken from my paternal grandfather's album the Viceroy Lord Curzon and Lady Curzon make sure their guests the Duke and Duchess of Connaught are comfortable in their howdah on the elephant on the right.

Daddy with some Gurkhas on the padang, *the parade ground, in Kuala Lumpur. There can seldom have been sharper creases on shorts.*

I never asked my father why he joined the Gurkhas. There were many other Indian regiments at the time. Like all who applied to become Gurkha officers you had to learn to speak Gurkhali first. You had to serve six months in another British regiment first (which one, Daddy? Why didn't I ask or make a note?) and then you were catapulted in at the deep end. Jimmy's first tour of duty was on the North West Frontier, with a hundred fighting-fit Nepali soldiers who thought nothing of running up sheer mountains with a full pack on their back. Daddy loved the Gurkhas completely: he loved their bravery and humour, their modesty and wicked sense of fun. As soldiers they had,

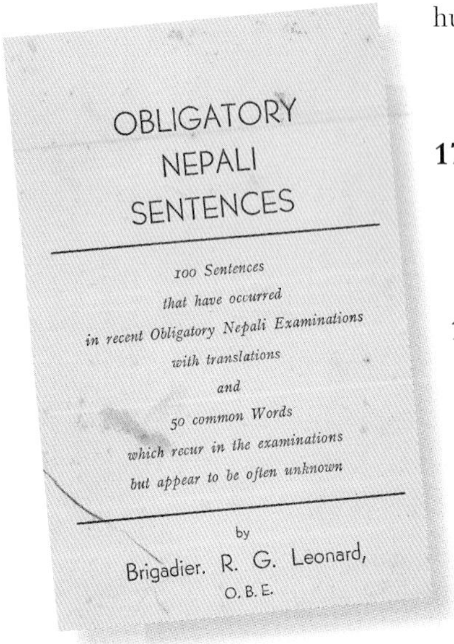

OBLIGATORY
NEPALI
SENTENCES

100 Sentences
that have occurred
in recent Obligatory Nepali Examinations
with translations
and
50 common Words
which recur in the examinations
but appear to be often unknown

by
Brigadier. R. G. Leonard,
O. B. E.

17. Dailo thunieko thiyo ani tala bata ragat bagdai aundai thiyo
The door shut and blood streamed out from below

19. Jahan sukai gaye pani gaun ma mareko manchhe matrai phela paren
Wherever I went I came across dead men only in the village

41. Tetikheri mero ghar khatkera ma Silkkim ma saryo
Then my house fell down and I moved to Sikkim

These rather gruesome phrases were important to learn for the Obligatory Nepali Examination: you had to pass to be allowed into a Gurkha regiment.

6
GURKHA RIFLES

My father, very young. He had only just joined the regiment as a second-lieutenant.

The Gurkha soldier is never without his kukri; the legend is that, having been drawn from its sheath, it has to see blood before it goes back. Certainly it strikes terror into the hearts of anyone who has the misfortune to come up against it.

and have, no equals in the world and are feared, respected and loved by all who come into contact with them.

The Second World War had started when my parents met, in Srinagar where Grandpa Weir was Resident at the time; Jimmy would have been on leave. Srinagar, capital of Kashmir, is sublimely beautiful. Great lakes are surrounded by Himalayan mountains, kingfishers dip and flash in the water, huge plane trees, *chinars*, cast cooling shadows in the hot summer months; and the hard, snowy winters give way to spring with all the flowers of paradise bursting from the cold ground. On the lakes are houseboats, enormous moored wooden palaces reached by *shikaras*, little gondolas propelled by paddles shaped like hearts. No wonder people fell in love there; no wonder my parents spent their honeymoon there in 1941, on a houseboat moored on the Dal Lake. When Srinagar became too hot the British retreated to Gulmarg, an alpine resort reached only on foot or on horseback. High up in the pine forests were long wooden bungalows called 'huts'. Granny and Grandpa Weir had a hut up there; there were picnics and dances, golf tournaments and hill-walking to make a holiday complete and unforgettable. Now a road has been built up to Gulmarg and coaches filled with tourists make the slow steep journey upwards, to Nedou's Hotel and the Golf Course. There is a ski lift too; a changed and crowded place. Everywhere changes. The Buddhists say the only thing in life you can be absolutely certain of is change.

Jimmy was a very good horseman and often rode in point-to-points. Here he receives a handshake and a cup. Everyone had dogs in those days and when they rode out with their assorted hounds it was called a 'bobbery pack'.

My father sent an assortment of photographs to his mother in England, probably writing the details on the back of each picture, as this is my grandmother's hand. She stuck them all into an album which was eventually passed down to me.

SELF ON MY 7/8 CHARGER COLORADO

Lhasa
Tibet.

August 21st. 1930

THE RESIDENCY
GANGTOK

My darling Beatrice

This letter will I hope go by air m[…]
& it will have come a long journey – first on [a]
cooly's back all the way from here to the trai[n]
at Kalimpong Road Station (where we met Pa[…]
that day do you remember?)

Well, we have been here for a fortnight n[…]
& I have met lots of […] Tibetan ladies [&]
[…] naturally sm[…]
wear wonderful silk […]
themselves with jewel[s …]
but as they wear […]
never run about or […] look
wouldn't like that […] for […]
important all the […]
real good walks o[…] me

It is lovely here in […] pro[…]
we stay for another month. which […]
shall do. only it will be cold going dow[n]
Gangtok through Southern Tibet and
passes in October. W[e …]

Daddy dressed for dinner at King's House with the Templers in Kuala Lumpur. He was ADC to General, later Field Marshal, Sir Gerald Templer, High Commissioner to the Federated Malay States.

Mummy in Hong Kong. When we were there the tallest building was four stories high.

A letter from Granny to Beatrice, my mother, who was ten and at boarding school in England. Granny describes a long visit to Lhasa; she and Mummy's elder sister Joan Mary made wonderful drawings of all they saw, while my grandfather talked matters of state with the thirteenth Dalai Lama. Mummy grew up to love mountains almost more than anything in her life; she was at her happiest at the thought of a really gruelling trek.

These were called Polyphotos: nowadays they would be called contact sheets. These were taken in England when we were on leave: I must have been a year and a half.

I was born in Kashmir, in Srinagar, on the first day of May in 1946. My sister Aelene had been born two years before in Abbottabad, in present day Pakistan, and she could speak a little Urdu when we left India for good in 1947 but I was too young to speak or remember anything from that time. We sailed home to Southampton on the *Franconia*, and then started the journeying to and from the Far East by ship; the *Windrush*, the *Empire Orwell*, the *Dilwara*. Each trip took about a month to reach Singapore, five weeks if you were going to Hong Kong. We washed in tin baths in sea water and showered with fresh water to rinse away the salt. Every day we had an orange to eat: we looked forward to the Suez Canal where a pilot would be brought out to the ship by motor launch, nimbly climbing aboard on a lowered ladder to steer us through the canal's narrow banks into the Mediterranean, or, if we were going east, into the Red Sea. For two years we lived in Hong Kong; for three years we were stationed in Kuala Lumpur, where the Emergency was at its height, with communist terrorists moving down the Malay Peninsula to be fought off and repulsed by the Gurkhas amongst other troops. Malaya became my home utterly; I loved the sultry tropical heat, the vivid colours of flowers and birds, the sudden black thunderstorms and scarlet sunsets. My sister and I walked

Sitting on Grandpa Weir's lap in Hong Kong. They came to visit us before setting off for Kenya where their house at Karen had just been built.

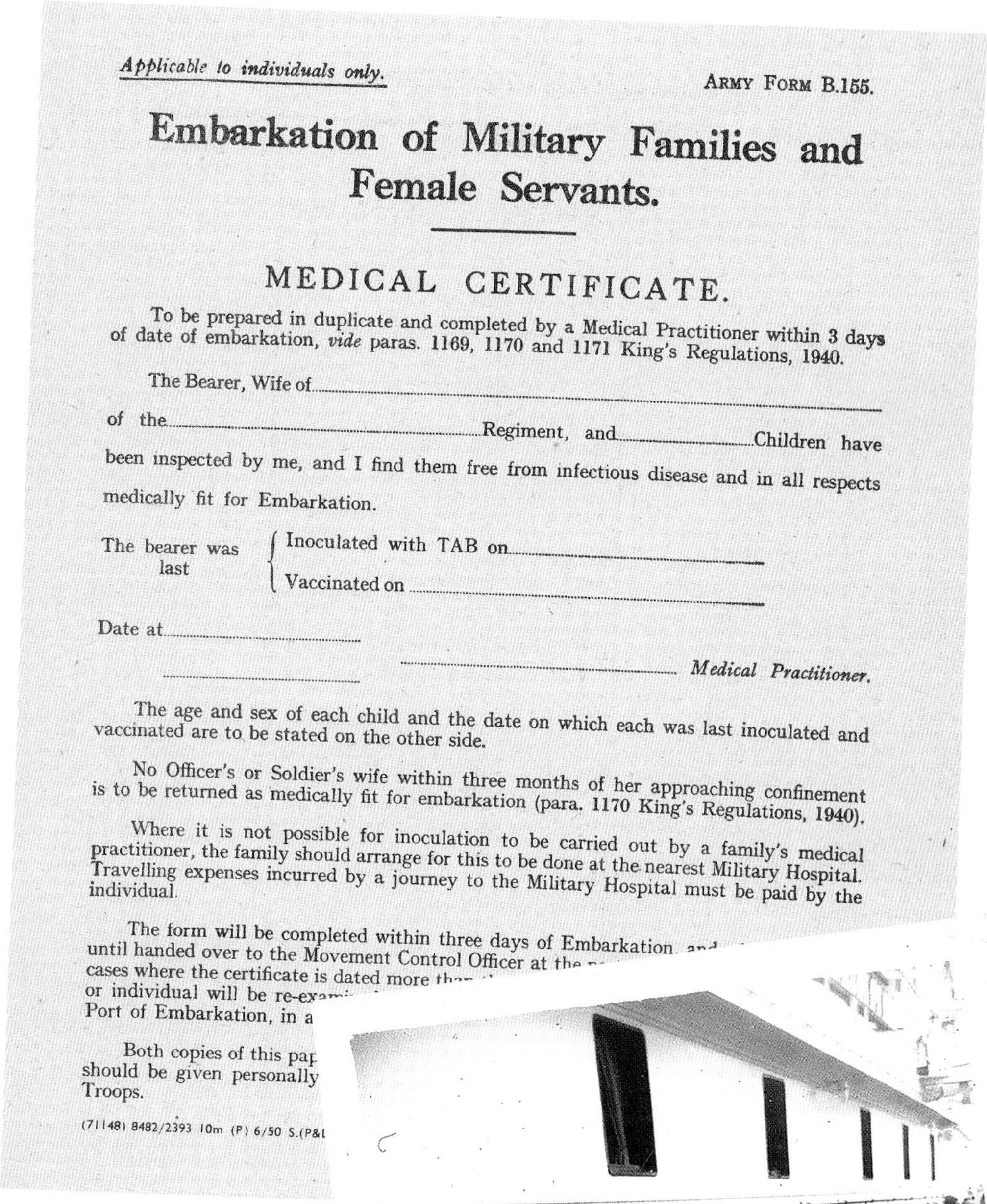

Applicable to individuals only.

ARMY FORM B.155.

Embarkation of Military Families and Female Servants.

MEDICAL CERTIFICATE.

To be prepared in duplicate and completed by a Medical Practitioner within 3 days of date of embarkation, *vide* paras. 1169, 1170 and 1171 King's Regulations, 1940.

The Bearer, Wife of..

of the..Regiment, and.......................Children have been inspected by me, and I find them free from infectious disease and in all respects medically fit for Embarkation.

The bearer was last { Inoculated with TAB on..
Vaccinated on..

Date at..............................

....*Medical Practitioner.*

The age and sex of each child and the date on which each was last inoculated and vaccinated are to be stated on the other side.

No Officer's or Soldier's wife within three months of her approaching confinement is to be returned as medically fit for embarkation (para. 1170 King's Regulations, 1940).

Where it is not possible for inoculation to be carried out by a family's medical practitioner, the family should arrange for this to be done at the nearest Military Hospital. Travelling expenses incurred by a journey to the Military Hospital must be paid by the individual.

The form will be completed within three days of Embarkation, and until handed over to the Movement Control Officer at the cases where the certificate is dated more th or individual will be re-exam Port of Embarkation, in a

Both copies of this pap should be given personally Troops.

(71148) 8482/2393 10m (P) 6/50 S.(P&L

On board ship; my sister is in charge of someone else's baby in the foreground; I am sitting on some lap in the middle. We were going to Hong Kong and it looks hot and sweaty. The ships were without frills; deck quoits and games of canasta were the high spots for grown-ups. Children attended on-board schools but we were exempt as my father used to devise lessons for us of reading and writing.

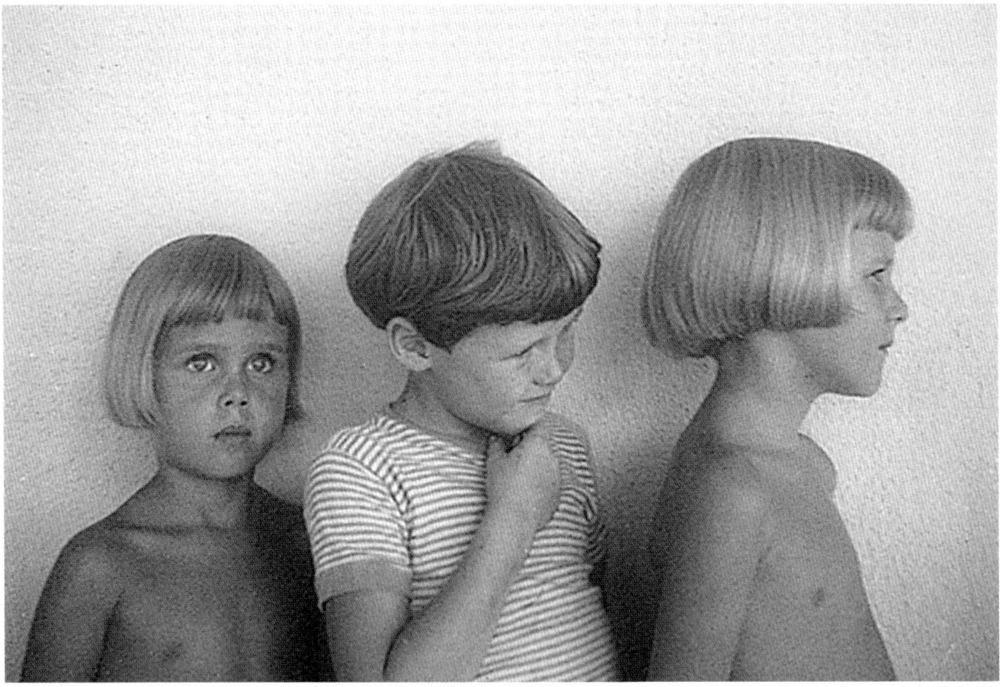

Our hair was cut into neat cool pudding basins. We were always brown from swimming but no-one sunbathed in the tropical heat: only mad dogs went out in the midday sun, not English children. In later life I overtook my sister in height but here I am still shorter by half a head.

each day to the Army School; travel was restricted and during school holidays if we went to cooler parts of the country like Fraser's Hill we had to drive in an armed convoy.

We lived in an army bungalow on the edge of a little airstrip. The garden was non-existent when we arrived but in the three years we were there my father planted trees and flowers and made a lawn from the tough saw-toothed grass called *lalang*. Our lives followed ordered paths: school at 8 o'clock, before the heat of the day came slamming down, until midday; then walk home on a rough road made of great chunks of crystal quartz, like stepping over diamonds as big as the Ritz; a siesta after lunch, a walk to the tin mines with the dog; mucking about on the verandah or playing the wind-up gramophone until supper; then bath, reading, bed with the night sounds of the Malayan creatures clicking and croaking through the closed shutters in the velvet blackness.

We always had some sort of animals: Judy, our golden laughing dog, had been abandoned at the Officers' Mess on Christmas Eve so she came home to us for ever, and Kinky, our imperturbable and placid cat had been rescued from drowning by my mother while we were walking the dog. There was an iguana for a short time, and three ducklings bought in the market to ease the strain on their basket, stuffed so full with the anxious little feathery bodies, but although I prayed every night I never got a pony (I never actually saw a pony in Malaya; and I only ever saw three sheep, and they looked like goats). A home without an animal was unthinkable.

The guinea pigs, Sammy and Michael, we kept on a balcony in the Hong Kong flat; by the time we got to Malaya we had Judy, our golden stray dog, and cats, of whom Kinky was the most senior. A friend's budgie on my head reminds me of the Egyptian bird-god Horus.

Daddy taught us to swim when we were tiny, and we swam almost every day.

My aunt Joan Mary drew my father and anyone who would sit still enough for her.

The Army School was good and we flourished. When I was six, I was cast in my first role as an actress. I played the Queen in an A.A. Milne poem: 'The King asked the Queen and the Queen asked the Dairymaid: "Could we have some butter for the Royal slice of bread?"'. Mummy made me a beautiful blue satin dress on her Singer sewing machine, and a golden cardboard crown. I was very nervous; but it was that moment, of being in the middle of a story with people listening and watching, that must have smuggled the thought into my mind that from then on I would be an actress.

The King died when we were in Malaya, and it was my father's job to organise the great parade in honour of the Coronation of Queen Elizabeth The Second. Oh! What medals and pencil-sharpeners we had! What mugs and handkerchiefs! It was exciting beyond belief as we had no real idea what London was like, or even where it was. We had the sketchiest concept of royalty, and no notion of smog or snow or good old British fish and chips. I was given a lead model of the golden Coronation State Coach, a thing it seemed to me of

The garden in HQ Malaya was shaping up; we had a gardener called a caboon, who scythed the grass and chewed betel nut with equal energy.

FEDERATION OF MALAYA
MALAYAN DRIVING LICENCE

Before we went to dancing classes we had to take salt tablets. My mother was learning to drive and felt that any speed over thirty miles an hour was recklessly dangerous, so journeys were quite sedate. I heard Offenbach's 'Barcarolle' for the first time in the big bungalow where we learned to point our toes and dance the waltz; that music always reminds me of hot dark afternoons, with a storm brewing and lizards on the walls.

unsurpassable beauty. I kept it for years. I may still have it. There was a Fancy Dress party for the children and we went as Norwegian girls (the Voyage of the Kon-Tiki was the book everyone was reading) in outfits made by Mummy on her trusty sewing machine. Our school dresses were made by her as well; and much later in life she was still making things, bed-jackets and jerseys, for friends and family and charity raffles. When it was time for us to go 'home' to England in 1954, the year after the Coronation, when our hair had grown down to our waists but was always worn in plaits, it was a sudden lurch into the unknown again; not exactly scaring, but bringing with it a slash of pain at what you must leave behind, friends, animals and my own beloved country, Malaya. We turned our faces to the west and set sail for Southampton for the last time, on the *Dilwara*, lying at anchor in Singapore's bustling harbour.

Norwegian girl, Queen in blue satin, wood-nymph, dancing girls and princesses with babies. Dressing up was a passion I have not lost to this day. Acting is just pretending to be someone else. We are all actors at some stage of our lives.

Early Days

Outside my aunt's farmhouse, my sister and I wear tunics for my first term at St Mary's. She has a girdle round her waist awarded for Deportment and Courtesy. My hair had just been cut rather savagely and never recovered its earlier childish lustre, not then, not ever.

The thrill of returning to England was vanquished at Southampton: cold and pitilessly grey, thin streaks of skylight spiking the huge arrival hangar, it seemed to me to be a pretty miserable place to call home. But I had reckoned without the staggering charm of late spring, and scented June days, and cuckoo song and roses in hedgerows. My sister and I were sent to board at a small school called Mickledene in the village of Rolvenden in Kent, where my parents eventually bought a house, and where my family lived until the turn of the century.

Mickledene was contained in a small farmhouse and a pair of oast-houses, for drying hops; their roundels had been converted to circular classrooms, and morning assembly was held in what had been a long low barn. Only a few children boarded, and there were three little dormitories called Early Lights, Middle Lights and Late

Boarders' House, Mickledene.

Some postcards demonstrating the bonuses of Mickledene School. The heavy scent of summer roses and the scrubby grass take me back to playing after classes were over before the boarders went in for tea. The bedrooms were cold but I soon got used to them. In the middle bed I dreamed I had a pony of my own. The classrooms stored and exuded the terrifying smell of cabbage, known and dreaded in schools across the nation.

A Bedroom, Mickledene.

Kindergarten, Mickledene.

School House from Playing field, Mickledene.

My writing aged nine; my parents were saddened by this style of hand-writing. Later I changed to a more italicised way of writing. The 'X marks the spot' can be checked in the first postcard shown on the page before this.

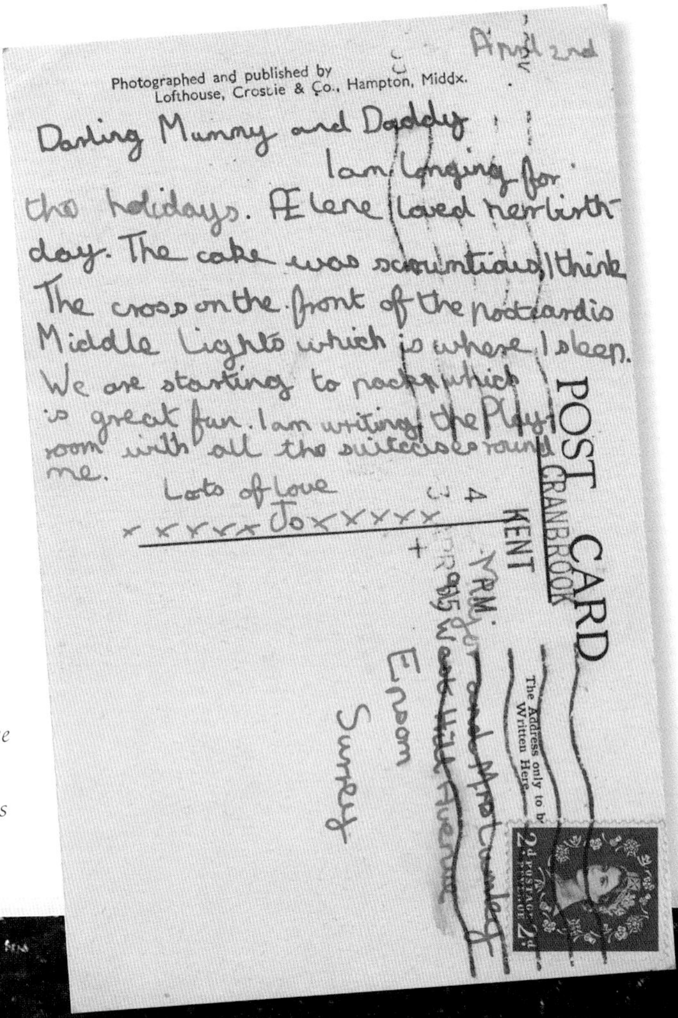

April 2nd

Photographed and published by
Lofthouse, Crostie & Co., Hampton, Middx.

Darling Mummy and Daddy
I am longing for the holidays. Ælene loved her birthday. The cake was scrumtious. I think The cross on the front of the postcard is Middle Lights which is where I sleep. We are starting to pack which is great fun. I am writing in the Playroom with all the suitcases round me.
Lots of Love
x x x x x Jo x x x x x

POST CARD
The Address only to be Written Here

Mr. and Mrs Lumley
95 West Hill Avenue
Epsom
Surrey

Sports day at Mickledene. Jacky Binns kneeling holds a tiny silver cup. I am wearing black gym shoes on the left. Mary Steele is standing to Jacky's right. She came on to St Mary's too, where she continued to look rather marvellous in whatever she had to wear.

Lights. Lordy! It was cold in those narrow iron beds. Homesickness was a new and unfamiliar demon, and seemed worse when you were longing not just to escape from school but to wish yourself back in a country half a world away, hot steamy Malaya with its monsoons and moonflowers and the clicketty-clack of the Chinese playing Mah-Jong. We learned Shakespeare and French, horrible Maths and lovely Art. We made Mothering Sunday cards and calendars and wrote essays about imaginary islands and wild horses. We were taught to write in rather loopy cursive hand, very inferior to italics, which give you a better template from which you might write clearly, quickly and attractively.

My father had a brief stint in the War Office and we were posted to Epsom; every Sunday we wrote from school to our parents, and walked the mile to church in the village; sometimes we listened to songs on the gramophone, 'The Ugly Duckling' and the 'Isle of Capri', 'Love and Marriage' and 'Che Sera, Sera'. At the end of term we bundled into cars or trains and sped off, to holidays with uncles and aunts, sometimes at Epsom where my mother yearned for the mountains, sometimes in Kent at Court Lodge Farm, where my aunt Joan Mary and her husband Ivor Jehu had bought a farm when they left India. We never had holidays as such, we simply went home from school and that was the holidays. If you did things, it was going to point-to-points or the sea-side at Jury's Gap, or a bike ride in the lanes or just mucking about. We never had school holiday projects, and they seem to this day to be

Maybe, on the right, is our only girl cousin. In the holidays we mucked about most of the time, including trespassing into Dougie's Barn where we lit paraffin lamps to give us light amongst the straw bales. I truly believe in guardian angels.

With Mary 'Bony' Hammond, outside the sixth form common room, Pilgrim's Progress. All our rooms were named after holy places, like Bethesda and Carmel, or after letters in the Greek alphabet: Kappa, Lamda, Sigma, Alpha and Epsilon. Bony and I did 'A' level German together, and we were prefects and in the first lacrosse team.

Below: a lacklustre report. My sympathy for the teaching profession knows no bounds.

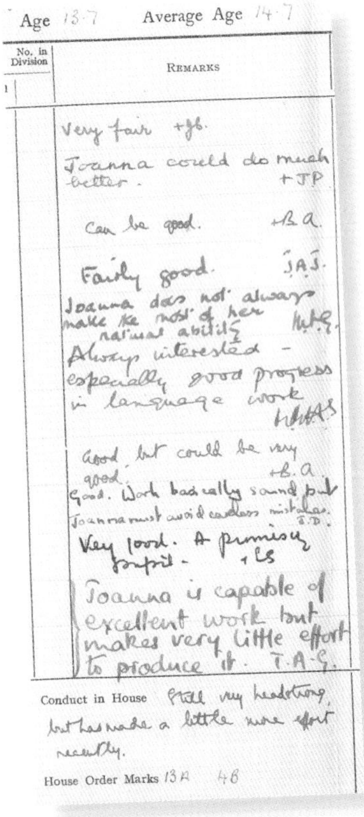

Age 13·7 Average Age 14·7

No. in Division	Remarks
1	Very fair +JB.
	Joanna could do much better. +JP
	Can be good. +B.a.
	Fairly good. JAS.
	Joanna does not always make the most of her natural ability. MKG
	Always interested – especially good progress in language work. [illegible]
	Good but could be very good. +B.a.
	Good. Work basically sound but Joanna must avoid careless mistakes. S.D.
	Very good. A promising pupil. +LS
	Joanna is capable of excellent work but makes very little effort to produce it. T.A.G.

Conduct in House Still very headstrong but has made a little more effort recently.

House Order Marks 13A 46

the essence of awfulness, having to think of school every day of the holidays, having to write some ghastly diary or essay, or do sums, or read about the Industrial Revolution when you should be lazing about or dreaming or doing non-school things.

I left Mickledene when I was eleven to go to St Mary's, a convent on the ridge behind Hastings, run by a teaching order of Anglo-Catholic nuns called the Community of the Holy Family. Perhaps because I was three years older, or had got used to the life of a boarder, maybe because the building was so huge in comparison with Mickledene, I felt at home at once and loved my six years there.

There were two hundred girls in the school and of those about seventy boarded. My parents had had to go back to Malaya so Aelene and I spent holidays with friends and relations, and our weekly letters home were now addressed to Depot the Brigade of Gurkhas, Sungei Patani, Malaya. Letters from them to us would be collected from our pigeon-holes after breakfast on Monday mornings, read hastily and stuffed into the blazer pocket with leaking pens, string and sometimes a live mouse. (My mouse was called Reepicheep and a daygirl got her for me: I kept her with my socks and pants in the chest of drawers in the dormitory, which began to smell quite like a dungeon despite the wide-open windows and the gales blowing in past the rhododendrons and pine trees.)

Food was fairly spartan; twenty eggs cracked onto a tray and left for an hour in the oven so that they had to be torn and skewered from the blackened metal was Sunday breakfast after Early Service. We went to chapel often but it became quite normal for us in no time, summoned by bells, running from class to chapel and back, changing for games, clearing away the plates and doing the washing up in the huge echoing pantries with two tea towels to dry up seventy plates and tin forks. We used to go to chapel three times a day, sometimes more. We wore chapel veils, like large handkerchiefs tied over our hair with ribbons, which we were supposed to keep neatly folded so that they could be accessed at a moment's notice, probably for emergency praying. My friend Anthea somehow contrived to semi-destroy every item of clothing as soon as it was put in her ownership, so her crumpled veil was often covered with blotches of ink or grey smudges from pencil sharpenings. Other friends, like Mary Steele and Patricia Summerfield, looked good in whatever they wore, and seemed to grow into the right womanly shape without too much trouble. I was tall, with frizzy hair, spots, unfashionably broad shoulders and was a bit of a lout in retrospect. I don't remember us grieving very much about the way we looked, however: food was poor and so was our skin, but we laughed all the time and slept like the dead and dreamed of becoming gorgeous later.

Ten prefects and the head girl. Left to right, from the back row: Susan Young, Mary Hammond, Kate Crosthwaite, Elizabeth 'Dizzy' Duncan, Sally Hayes, me: in the front, Cordelia Cargill, Pippa Swain, Rosemary Andrew, Gillian McMurray and Jane Strickland. My prefect's badge had been temporarily removed for cigarette-related offences. I wonder if I have spelt all their once-unforgettable names correctly.

The school steps to the terrace, with us looking as lovely as we could. Sugar-stiffened petticoats under summer dresses: the bell about to ring for prep. Not a care in the world.

Being a junior girl in 4B was the best fun in the world: you had no responsibilities, the whole term ahead before your parents would read your school report, a fine array of older girls and prefects to cheek and outwit, a mass of school work which was easy-peasy, woods and pathways winding through bamboo and chestnut trees, rhododendrons and wild garlic on the way to the games field, wood pigeons cooing and floorboards squeaking with the drumming feet of girls in Clarks shoes thumping off to their next assignment. There were too many of us, though: the Babyboomers had arrived, children born the year after the Second World War had ground to its terrible conclusion. The intake into the lowest class when I arrived was forty, not twenty as usual: so we were split up into parallel classes for a year. After that a dreadful thing happened: some of us were skimmed off the top of the form and pushed up a year. I was one of the 'lucky ones' and I never recovered. Because I had always relied on my photographic memory and animal cunning I had always found school work simple (except maths, which trips me up to this day. I can't dial a number without saying it out loud, but am preternaturally gifted at getting roughly the right answer while top bankers flounder). Suddenly we were expected to have absorbed a year's learning in a term and I am afraid I stopped in my tracks and failed from then on. From having come top in most subjects I was now nowhere and I stopped caring too. My bad behaviour attracted many order marks and punishments, some of which were learning poems. Excellent: I could do that in a trice. There was always the school play and the choir, Games, Art and English, French, Latin and German and Italian (lovely languages! I love a language) and fascinating Biology and brow-crumpling Chemistry, History a mystery as I read books like *The Robe* and *Gone With the Wind* under the desk, and Geography with maps of islands to be outlined in Caran D'Ache Azure Blue.

A wide hairband was a fruitless way of trying to tame my very bad hair. Expression hoping to emulate Claudia Cardinale, as I knew Brigitte Bardot was well beyond reach at this stage.

Second right: I try to look like Aaron in the school play. Adetoun Fagbayi and Aronke Alade hold peacock fans, and Imogen Newbatt, heavily bearded and our version of Judi Dench, played Moses in Christopher Fry's Firstborn. *I went on playing men, and got used to wearing moustaches. Much later in life, Patsy emerged as having been a man for a spell in her chequered past.*

The Sisters of the Holy Community were exceptional women. They had the pastoral care of a large number of girls and yet they had never been parents themselves. They took no hostages and what they said, went: but I don't remember any nun being unkind or unfair. On the contrary, they were miraculously even-tempered and good humoured, full of enthusiasm and encouragement; their minds were always on their own calling, the selfless service of their Saviour, and their vows were threefold then, as they are now: poverty, chastity and obedience, symbolized by the three knots worn in the girdle round their waists. They owned nothing. Their blue bedspreads would become their coffin covering, their food was what we wouldn't eat (not much, despite much of it being really grim) and their comforts were few. Sister Elizabeth sometimes kept sweets in her long pocket which swung under her grey floor-length habit, and in the summer when they thought no-one was looking they would roll up their skirts and play cricket. Terms passed, and juniors became seniors and I was eventually made a prefect ('Set a thief to catch a thief' said Sister Jesse succinctly). Inexorably responsibilities mounted up, lists had to be made and registers taken, rules were to be enforced and miscreants to be punished, and suddenly the poacher had become game-keeper.

Looking back it strikes me how often in our lives we start again from scratch. At no stage of my grown-up life have I wielded the power we

Fiddling about with my Slazenger racquet in a tennis match. Is that Caroline Moule as my partner? Amazingly I got colours for netball, lacrosse and tennis despite being uncompetitive and fairly lazy due to trying to look cool in front of junior girls. It was considered rather a poor show to be seen to be trying too hard at games.

Summer dress and blazer outside Pilgrim's Progress. Hair now trapped in a beehive of sorts. I must have been sixteen. The school gardens were huge and shady and sunny and full of secret corners.

On the lawn at Sparkeswood, the house my parents bought when my father left the Army. Signs of flower power are showing in my headband with blossoms tucked in. My father would wear any old hat he found in the hall. He loved gardening, but got to the stage where he couldn't bear to kill any living thing, even daisies and buttercups, by cutting the grass.

had as prefects, swishing about in our pleated skirts and twinsets like middle-aged women, demanding respect and subservience. You start school as a baby aged five and leave aged seventeen going on sixty. Then you start again in the wide, wide world as a green and innocent beginner, behaving like a child, with new boyfriends and hair in bunches and immature thoughts about how the world should be run ('Let's share everything! Let's stay up all night and not pay taxes! Let's go round the world like gypsies and never settle down in boring jobs!') and slowly the world turns and suddenly you are struggling with forms to fill in and bills to pay. Your own children grow, and eat like wolves, and life seems like hard work with none of the rewards you thought would come your way simply by being a grown-up. Then comes the time to retire, and back you go again, holding hands on the beach and laughing as you eat apples with your dentures firmly attached by glue to your gums; sometimes television shows geared for the very young are more appealing than the alien humour and scary news programmes that make up the menu in the listings. Then, as Shakespeare noted, we are back to being big babies again, balding and in need of care and changing and feeding, and one day, so soon that you may be able to see the beginning of your life at the same time, the end comes, and That's All There Was. There has to be a way of looking at it to make a story, to make sense of it.

How we longed to be like the film stars of those days! We dipped our nylon petticoats in sugar-water and dried them on radiators to make them stiff so our skirts would stick out like Brigitte Bardot's pink gingham dress. Bardot! But her baby-ish pout and bed-time hair said Young Creature, not svelte siren of forty. Even then, women were beginning to try to look young, rather than mature. True, Sophie Loren looked utterly *femme fatale* but she was not our icon, nor was Marilyn Monroe with her curves and thick lipstick. It was Bardot then and still is now, fifty years later. And just as my school days were drawing to a close, the Beatles arrived with Love Me Do (Oh! How thrilling! I do love you, mop-top charmers from Liverpool even though I have never really been anywhere in Britain except school and the south. I love you, and I love the thought of London, waiting huge and wicked like a distant stalker with sweets). The pantheon of Buddy Holly and the Everly Brothers, Little Richard, Cliff and even Elvis had to be reshuffled so that the new world order of pop music could accommodate the irresistible and magnetic cheeky-boys. Shimmering behind them, almost coming into focus, was the New World, of flower power and mini-skirts, and streets paved with promises. I would fit in there: somehow I would fit in there nicely.

When I left school I joined the family in Italy on the first holiday we had ever had. Schooldays faded away like footprints in the sand and the idea of what to do to earn money had not yet crossed my mind. I was inching nearer to my dream of being mistaken for a French woman whilst wearing sunglasses and nail varnish, the acme of sophistication. Still reading: always reading (and what looks like drinking too).

Make-up & Mini-skirts

Boots: 'model's own', but we didn't say that in those days. These yellow boots from Biba were my favourites and look a bit shabby in the picture through constant wear. It was expensive to buy shoes just for photographs: no models were rich enough to do that. Today you would never be expected to accessorise your own shots.

The flat we moved into in 1964 was just off the Earl's Court Road. It was on the fourth floor with no lift, and four of us shared it: Nina, Dinx, Aelene and me, squashed into two bedrooms, with a rented gas stove and no fridge. Paradise! I have never felt quite the same thrill as waking at dawn to scurry off to my first ever modelling job at the department store Debenham and Freebody, hearing the muffled announcements of the Underground station which roared away far below, seeing the scruffy rooftops and dusty pigeons and slapping on make-up by candlelight so that I wouldn't wake the others sleeping. After a month of training at Lucie Clayton I had been taken on as a model, just as skirts were creeping up above the knee and no-one, my dear, but no-one wanted to be seen without false eyelashes. (Actually, only models wore them at the time: but it is very easy, in your enthusiasm and excitement, to believe that the WHOLE WORLD cares about your new shade of eye-shadow, and will be watching every step of your mock-Courreges boots as you patter past shops called Carrot on Wheels and Granny Takes a Trip, hair in rollers under a headscarf, a man's watch weighing down your skinny wrist, pale-lipsticked mouth shouting 'Taxi!!!' as you race from job to job.)

London was on fire with excitement. A new Labour Government had been elected, the Keeler affair was recent history, the music and fashion and drop-dead fabness of the city was matched nowhere on earth, or so it seemed to us. True, as models we weren't paid a king's ransom but it was a great deal more than most people earned. It was considered very vulgar to talk about money in those days, so if you had it you picked up the tab and kept quiet. If you didn't, and were as skint as boracic lint, you dressed extravagantly in home-altered clothes, and made your own self into a work of art, or at least individuality, with necklaces and headbands, frills, hats, sunglasses and serious posing. Looking back at these pictures,

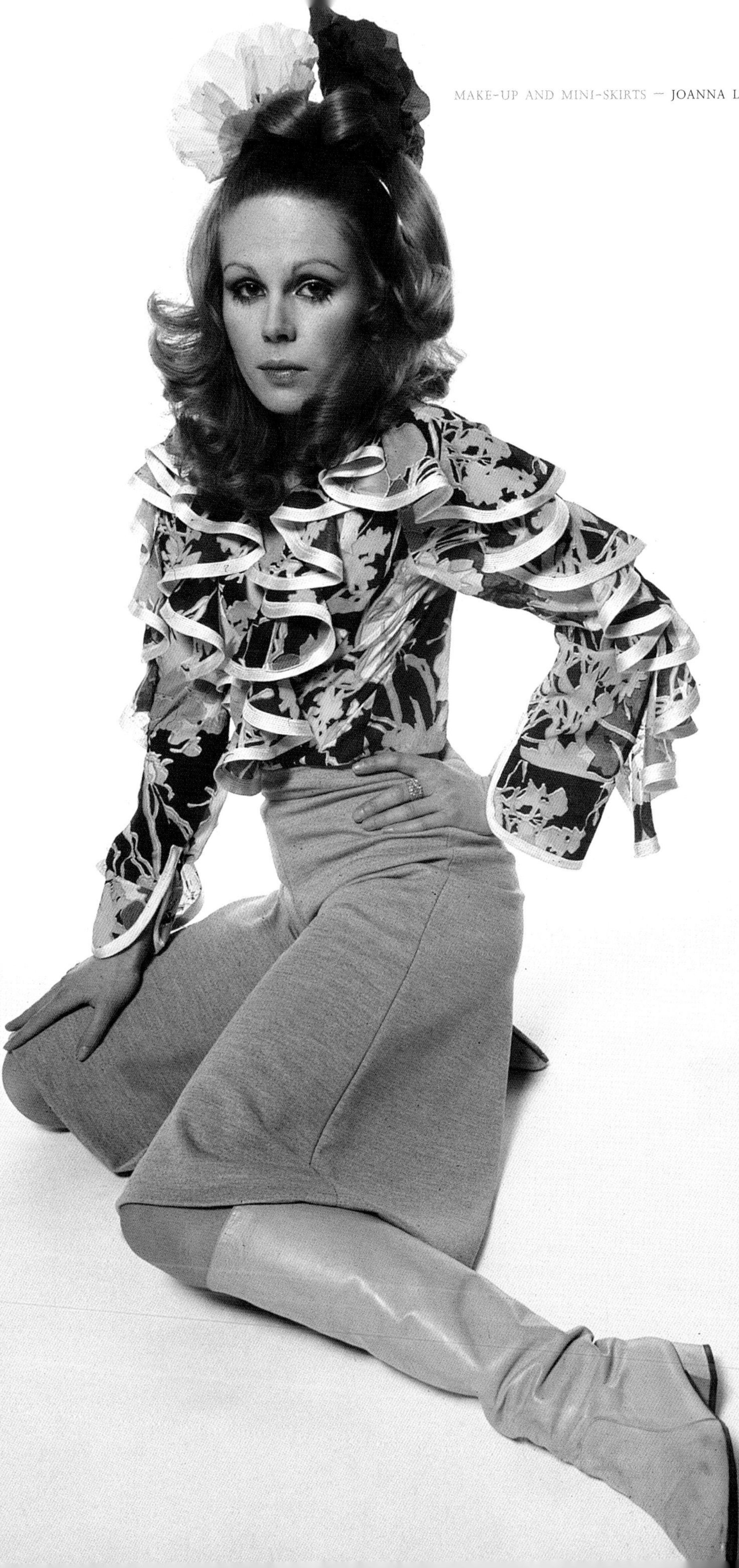

87

JOANNA LUMLEY

Height	5' 8"	Hauteur	173
Bust	34"	Poitrine	86
Waist	24"	Taille	61
Hips	35"	Hanches	89
Shoes	5	Chaussures	38
Gloves	7	Gants	7
Hair	Dark Blonde	Cheveux	Blonds Fonces
Eyes	Blue-Grey	Yeux	Bleu-Gris

HEADSHOT BY VIC SINGH–FULL LENGTH SHOT BY CLIVE ARROWSMITH

LUCIE CLAYTON 01-629 0667/8

We had model cards giving our statistics, with flattering photographs to show how good we could look. My size 5 feet were sometimes crammed into smaller shoes: the ones worn with thick white socks were actually size three. But it was for Queen *magazine, photographed by Clive Arrowsmith, so who was complaining.*

I wonder: how did I manage to pull it off? I didn't even have a hair-dryer. In the flat, we shared our clothes, tights and shoes and bags... we put one pound each into the kitty every week and scraped by on bread and cheese, as happy as skylarks, walking if we couldn't afford the bus or tube. Three years later, I had my own Mini (given in lieu

Below: in the kitchen at Earl's Court, with Nina and her then boyfriend, now husband, Hamish. We aimed to look like doped existentialists: the walls and floor were gloss yellow and I was clearly longing to look like an actress suffering from strangeness. Serious posing. Taken by my boyfriend Michael.

Sometimes (left) I posed with statues and furniture. Look at the length of the skirt. In Paris I was nearly arrested for my abbreviated hemline.

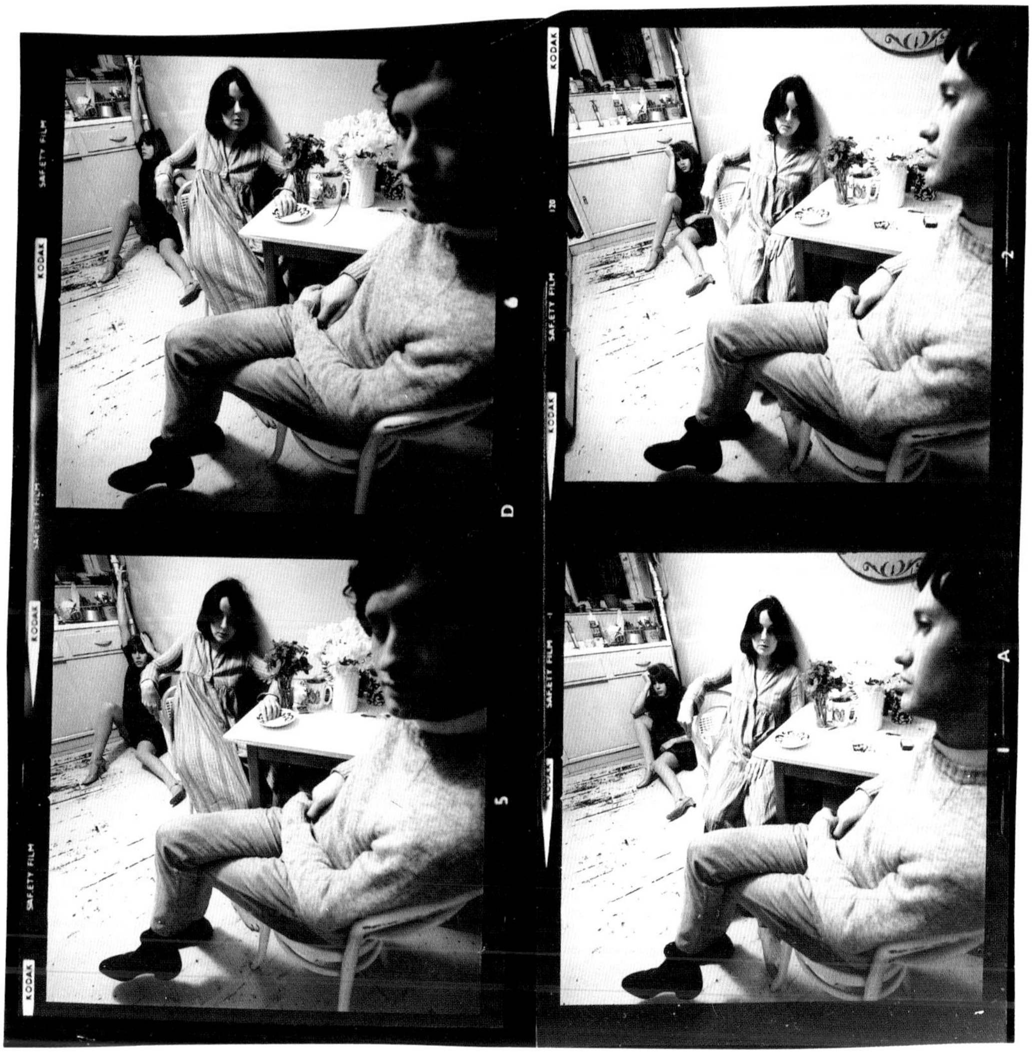
KODAK
SAFETY FILM

Focus on new Britain. Focus on young designers. Focus on the 21 Shops. Now strategically placed all over Britain. At WOOLLANDS, Knightsbridge. At Marshall & Snelgrove, Oxford Street W1, New Street, Birmingham, and now St. Anne's Place, Manchester, also Williams & Hopkins, Bournemouth. Dynamic young fashion ideas. Quick! Look what's in now. Wow!
Catching the mood
a long hot sum
C&A
Well, it just had to come... the little plastic dress
The craze for PVC has reached its zenith. We've had plastic macs, boots, bags and hats, now comes the plastic dress. This jokey little dress is great for the girl who zooms around at such a rate she doesn't have time for ironing. It's great for any mother with sticky-fingered children. When it gets dirty you just sponge it down. Available at the end of the week. C. & A. 39s. 11d.
onore
PAGE 8
FEMAIL
These shoes
How w
'Top Twelve' by
Here the
greatest
Harell
fashio
store
Ask
the
es
oaks

es for a town wife
Don't get caught
the rain...
DAILY MAIL, Wednesday, May 11, 1965
THE SUNDAY TELEGRAPH NOVEMBER 28, 1965
Join the chain gangs on the beach
BY LIZ ATKINSON
39s. 11d.
42s.
£5 10s.
Soft...Soft...Soft...that's the Vedonis feeling

WHAT IS A MODEL?

Second in Veronica Scott's series on the new models: Joanna Lumley

Extravagant prints, off-beat colours—*these are Jo Lumley's formulae for dressing-up clothes (which, after all, aren't intended to be overlooked!) Persian print Banlon trouser suit, Hildebrand, 10-14, 10½ gn.*

Likes unusual styles based on peasant themes that people notice. *Born under Taurus, Jo's extrovert, articulate —and her clothes are vivid too. Mexican smock and headscarf, printed cotton, comes from Granny Takes a Trip at World's End, Chelsea, 6½ gn. Openwork, natural colour, straw picture hat, Eaton Bag Co., 1 gn.*

JO LUMLEY, born in India twenty years ago, signed on with the Lucie Clayton model agency, began her modelling career in London by store modelling: 9-5.30, £8 a week.

First break came a few months later when a photographer asked her to pose for the cover of a book. It was never published, but it was her debut just the same. Today she's a regular WOMAN favourite.

With the same photographer she went to Moscow to photograph five fur coats in six days—a leisurely routine compared with her hectic photographic trips for catalogues.

Jo is a natural mimic and story-teller, recounting films, books and playing all parts like a full dramatic cast. She wants to be a film director. Vital, vulnerable, she is subject to thumping great fits of depression, dissecting and denigrating herself from head to toe—fat head, spotty face, prizefight shoulders, deformed ribcage, huge hips, bottle legs, tiny flipper feet—that's Jo, according to Jo. Actually, she is beautiful—warm, lively and womanly-looking. But she longs to be thin and can't stay that way. No wonder! She has a colossal schoolgirl appetite, consumes cheese by the pound (having given up sticky paste which she declares she "lived on" at school!).

Jo's "hung up" on ghosts and goblins, reads hands with sensational confidence and frequently calls everyone "Baby Doll" in fast-talking American.

Yet despite her exuberant nuttiness, Jo is full of the ingredients of the corny but very real "girl next door" who's always resolving a new fashion plan and always ending up with something else! Jo knows all the fashion rules, but she's Jo, and she dresses that way. Her fashion urges are original, chaotically colourful like she is—*and to my mind they prove that simple restrained elegance is not the be-all of the fashion story.*

There's a gaping place for *personal* experiment with colour, for impudent adventure in trying out unusual

22

The fashion for making dresses out of Indian bedspreads was at its height. This one came from Granny Takes a Trip. Heavy green-blue eyes lined with kohl, lime-green shift, scarlet PVC coat and rather saggy-fronted denim skirt with a jaunty John Lennon cap … that was what it was to be a model in 1965.

Woman – July 22 1967

Likes fine jersey shifts for day, *sleeveless or long sleeves. Must be very short, zip down back for quick dressing. Jersey dress, Simon Jeffrey, 10-14, 94s. 6d. Felt Cordoba, Edward Mann, 35s. 11d.* **Feels undressed without straps across her shoes.** *Shoes, Saxone, 2½-8½, 59s. 11d.*

styles; there's even room for mistakes if it's not the end of the piggybank.

Jo, stomping up the ruined, rocky Phoenician city of Solunto in Sicily in thick leather brogues plus huge lizard portmanteau handbag to pose in those "Persian" pantaloons at top of the page; Jo, swinging through the jam-packed streets of Palermo in Mexican smock and hat, left, to pose and show you her relaxwear, is a genuine original. Her fashion says so.

It may not be your style. But then, again, it may.

Next week: Newcomer Jenny Fussell

Prefers scruffy old clothes for weekends, *but picked this shadow-striped denim skirt with buttoned hip pockets, crepon shirt, PVC raincoat as having the suitable "knockabout" air. Skirt, Dorothy Perkins, 22-28 in. waist, 29s. 11d.; shirt, by Lewis Separates, 34-38 in. bust, 14s. 11d.; coat, Dunnimac, 10-14, 79s. 6d. Scarf, Aldbrook.*

23

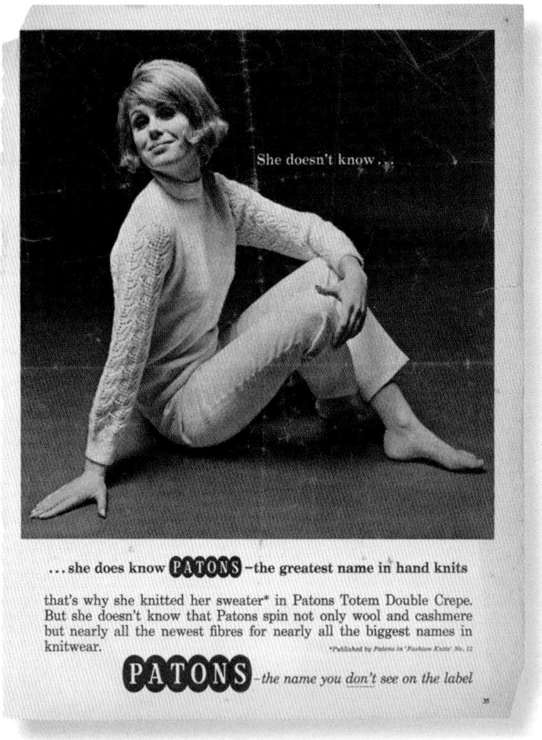
She doesn't know . . .
. . . she does know PATONS – the greatest name in hand knits
that's why she knitted her sweater* in Patons Totem Double Crepe. But she doesn't know that Patons spin not only wool and cashmere but nearly all the newest fibres for nearly all the biggest names in knitwear.
*Published by Patons in 'Fashion Knits' No. 12
PATONS – the name you don't see on the label
35

MORLEY
A clever co-ordination of stripes in varying widths makes a new twinset concept in 'Bri-Nylon'. Colours: orange fizz, parma, navy, spice. Sizes: 36-40 inches. Style Nos.: Sweater B 932, Cardigan B 933. Approximate retail prices: Sweater £2.9.6. Cardigan £2.19.6.
COLOUR CO-ORDINATES IN
BRI* NYLON
Facing page and inset: Pure white in 'Bri-Nylon' is crisply striped with self pattern and has matching ribbed knee socks. Colours: powder blue, white, carnation, green, daffodil, navy or coffee. Sizes: Sweater 36-40 inches. Stockings in medium and large. Style reference: Dandy. Approximate retail prices: Sweater £2.2.6, Stockings 5s 11d.

The roller-skating pictures were taken by one of the giants of the decade, David Montgomery. Tinka Patterson smiles past the diamonds at my ear; I grasp freezing steering wheels in a scrap yard (and later I was to be in Steptoe and Son *for real): and I do my best in nylon and wool. Thrilling.*

Only one of these girls will be able to . . .

Breakaway GIRLS HATE SNOBS–LOVE STEPTOE AND SON
To stun them in: ask any Breakaway girl what's cool in fibre kicks and she'll tell you Bri-Nylon chiffon. This gorgeously dotty dress weighs less than a bit of fluff–it's calculated to lift any girl out of the dumps. It's designed for evening shifts, but everyone would be thrilled to see her in it earlier.
'Who says I'm down in the dumps?'

Don't say a thing:
When thoughts are too deep for words, jewellery from Bensons speaks for you. It makes the great unmistakeable gesture. It's for keeps.
Bensons have been helping to express strong silent emotions in hard enduring stones for 126 years. People know it's the place to go when only the finest necklaces, rings, brooches, bracelets and watches will do. The necklace and the ring saying so much in the picture are diamonds set in platinum. Bensons, at 25 Old Bond Street, W1, are full of eloquent things.
just give her diamonds from Bensons

...stand still!
It's awful hard to stand still in Actionwear. Specially when the Actionwear has been tailored into slacks by Slimma. It's awful hard not to skate, slide, twist, twirl, wheel, whirl, flurry, hurry . . . when you're wearing slacks like these. Because Actionwear loves to move. And the Actionwear fabric springs back after anything. Yes, anything.
Slimma
Other colours; black, navy, red, pale blue, chocolate and dark green. Size 10 to 16. Price is 55/-
Actionwear
NYLON
CHEMSTRAND

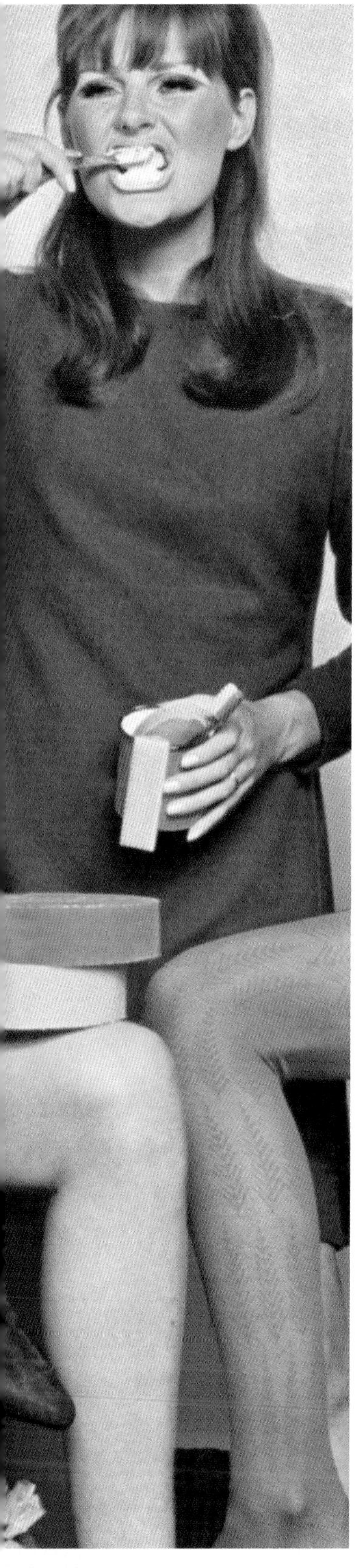

For the Daily Mail *'Rag Doll' series with a red rinse in the hair: in Duffy's shoot styled by Molly Parkin for the photographic spread Bailey said was the best of the year. Paulene Stone scrubs her teeth and I comb my red wig. These were daring and ground-breaking pictures at the time. And here I am again in frills and a wonky fringe.*

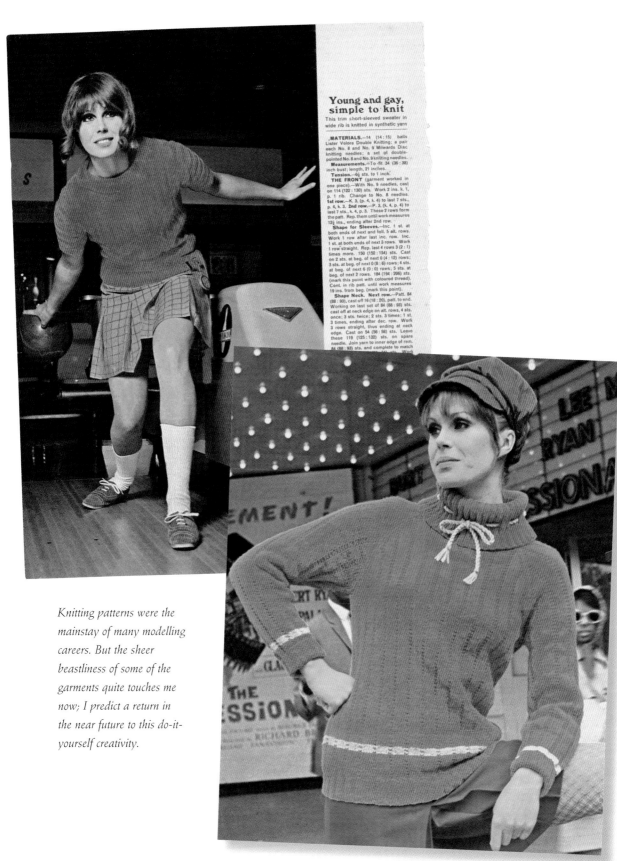

Young and gay, simple to knit

This trim short-sleeved sweater in wide rib is knitted in synthetic yarn

MATERIALS.—14 (14 : 15) balls Lister Velora Double Knitting; a pair each No. 8 and No. 9 Milwards Disc knitting needles; a set of double-pointed No. 8 and No. 9 knitting needles.

Measurements.—To fit 34 (36 : 38) inch bust; length, 21 inches.

Tension.—6½ sts. to 1 inch.

THE FRONT (garment worked in one piece).—With No. 9 needles, cast on 114 (122 : 130) sts. Work 2 ins. k. 1, p. 1 rib. Change to No. 8 needles. **1st row.**—K. 3, (p. 4, k. 4) to last 7 sts., p. 4, k. 3. **2nd row.**—P. 3, (k. 4, p. 4) to last 7 sts., k. 4, p. 3. These 2 rows form the patt. Rep. them until work measures 12½ ins., ending after 2nd row.

Shape for Sleeves.—Inc. 1 st. at both ends of next and foll. 5 alt. rows. Work 1 row after last inc. row. Inc. 1 st. at both ends of next 3 rows. Work 1 row straight. Rep. last 4 rows 3 (2 : 1) times more. 150 (152 : 154) sts. Cast on 2 sts. at beg. of next 0 (4 : 12) rows; 3 sts. at beg. of next 0 (8 : 6) rows; 4 sts. at beg. of next 6 (0 : 0) rows; 5 sts. at beg. of next 2 rows. 184 (194 : 206) sts. (mark this point with coloured thread). Cont. in rib patt. until work measures 19 ins. from beg. (mark this point).

Shape Neck. Next row.—Patt. 84 (88 : 93), cast off 16 (18 : 20), patt. to end. Working on last set of 84 (88 : 93) sts. cast off at neck edge on alt. rows, 4 sts. once; 3 sts. twice; 2 sts. 3 times; 1 st. 3 times, ending after dec. row. Work 3 rows straight, thus ending at neck edge. Cast on 54 (56 : 58) sts. Leave these 119 (125 : 132) sts. on spare needle. Join yarn to inner edge of rem. 84 (88 : 93) sts. and complete to match

EMENT!
LEE
RYAN
THE

Knitting patterns were the mainstay of many modelling careers. But the sheer beastliness of some of the garments quite touches me now; I predict a return in the near future to this do-it-yourself creativity.

A much later and more glamorous shoot on Mauritius with Patrick Lichfield. I worked with him more than almost any other photographer: he was amazingly good company, very funny, and charming to all he met. Here Jane Raphaely, fashion editor for South Africa's Fair Lady *magazine, steadies a glass of wine as we watch the* Sega *being danced by firelight on the beach. In the same shoot I sit with fruit and flowers, and listen to a sea-shell. I always longed for straight hair, never really achieved it.*

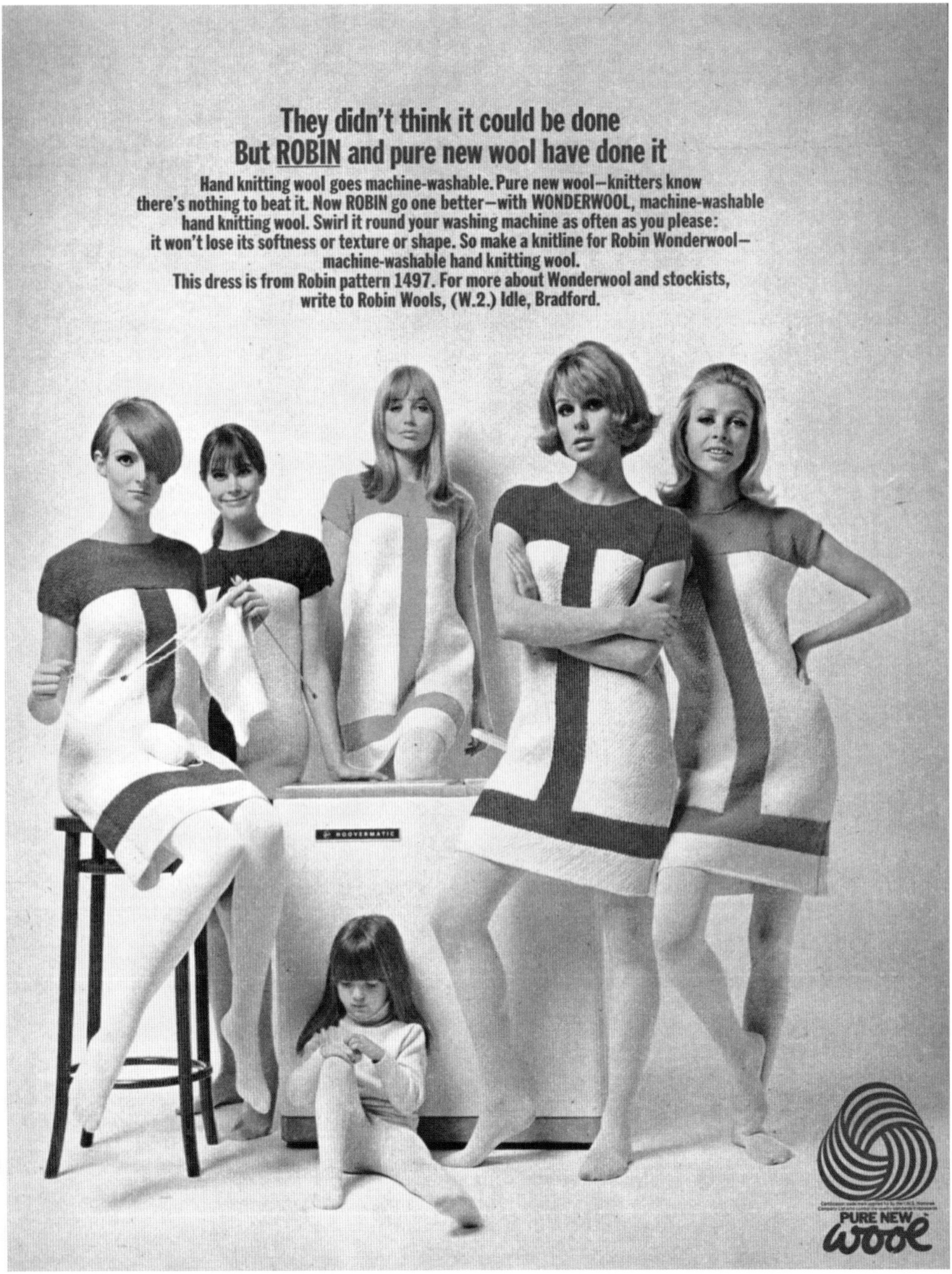
They didn't think it could be done
But ROBIN and pure new wool have done it
Hand knitting wool goes machine-washable. Pure new wool—knitters know
there's nothing to beat it. Now ROBIN go one better—with WONDERWOOL, machine-washable
hand knitting wool. Swirl it round your washing machine as often as you please:
it won't lose its softness or texture or shape. So make a knitline for Robin Wonderwool—
machine-washable hand knitting wool.
This dress is from Robin pattern 1497. For more about Wonderwool and stockists,
write to Robin Wools, (W.2.) Idle, Bradford.
PURE NEW
wool

Compare these two photographs: taken at different times and with different models, all except me. Below, Sue Murray, Sandra Paul, later Mrs Michael Howard, and Paulene Stone look gorgeous on a Rolls Royce while I, slightly lower-ranking and not as gorgeous, skulk behind on the bonnet. On the left, we look as though we are avatars of the picture on the right, all except Grace Coddington, Amazing Grace, now second in command at American Vogue, *the funky unpredictable short-haired knitter, the only model who could make a ball of yarn look cool. Jane Lumb in the centre in yellow is a dead ringer for Sue Murray in blue on the Rolls headlamp, with her arm bent to hide a rolled-over waistband. We were all almost interchangeable; almost, but utterly not. I was shelves behind any of these more famous faces. Happy as a clam to be in their company.*

To Her Majesty The Queen
Simpson (Piccadilly) Ltd

Admiration was reserved for those of us who could change our looks as much and as often as possible. Wigs and hairpieces were swapped and borrowed to give us New Looks. I found hair shoots chilling as hairdressers ('crimpers') sometimes misjudged just how much of a handful my hair was. It could stay up in the air if sprayed within an inch of its life, and they had no compunction about cutting bits off that they had failed to curl or set properly. I can truthfully say that my hair, and how it looks, has governed a large part of my professional life, as feeble as that sounds. Bad Hair Life is putting it too strongly: but the menace of the follicles is always with me. My hair will dance on my grave.

3

1 Joseph at Salon 33 makes a short centre parting; flicks the hair up at one side, and then divides the other side into near-ringlets

2 Using the same short parting, he catches one side of the hair into a short, fanned-out ponytail, and brushes the other side forward

3 At André Bernard, they're in love with the 1940s look. Stylist Colin uses big 1966 rollers to set a curly, wavy Rita Hayworth style

4 The same set is swooshed round into a curly "up" style. The hair is secured high on the left side, combed out into feathery curls

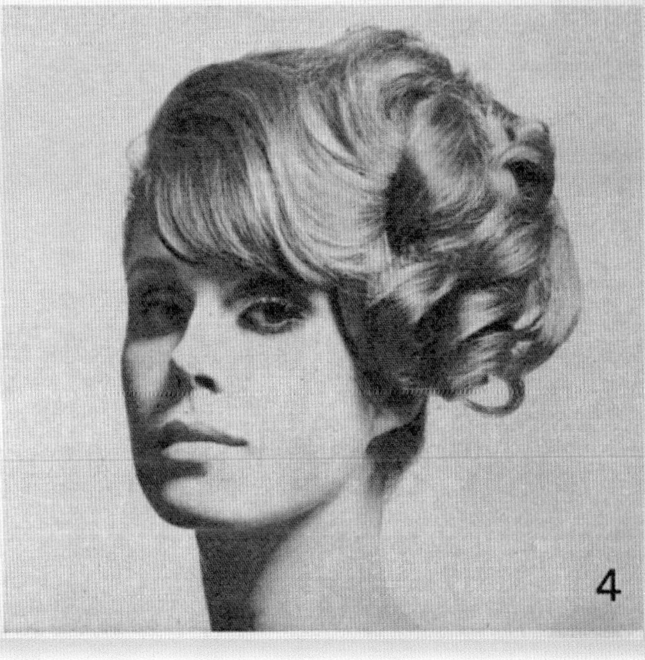

4

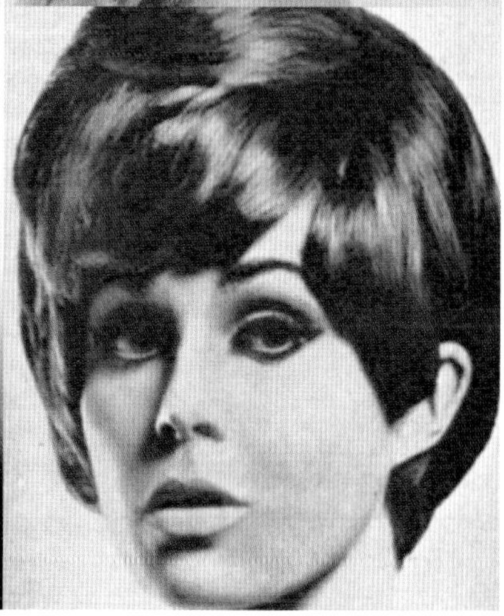

The kindest way of looking at these is to wonder if she could have made a career in espionage.

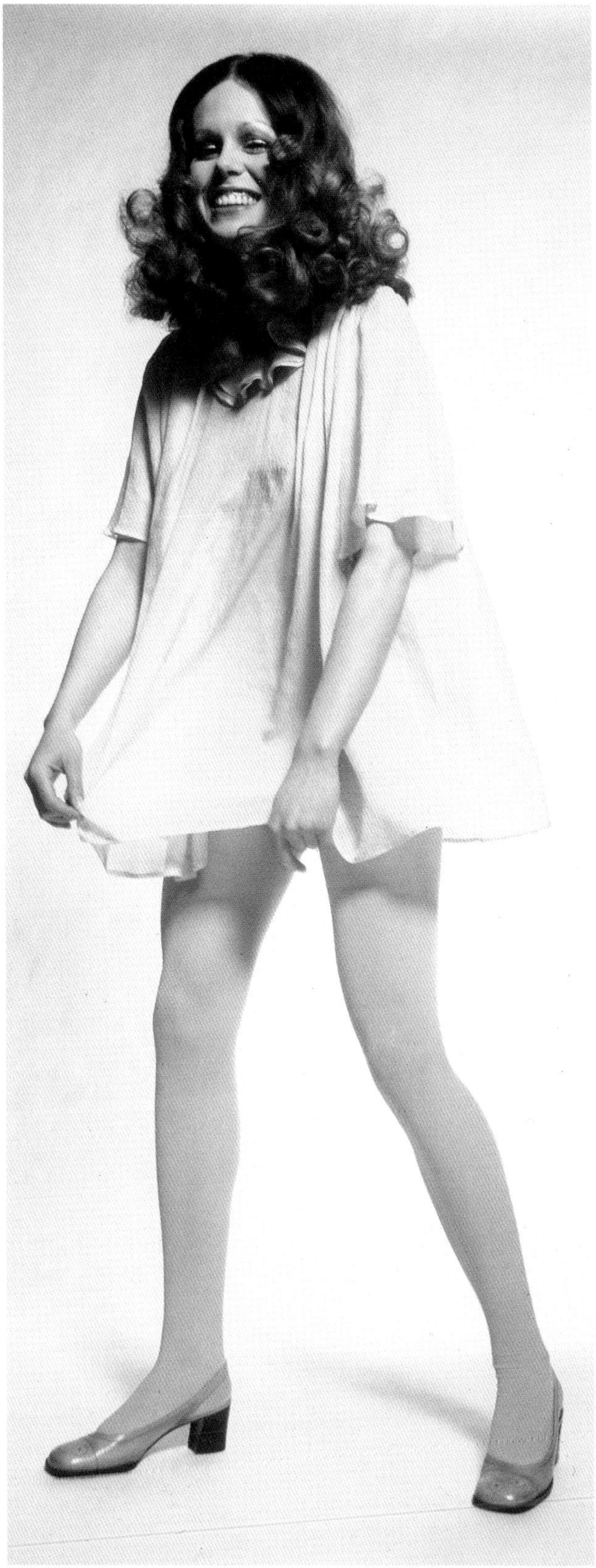

Yellow wig, black fright wig, clumps of hairpieces cunningly flopped onto the fringe, dyed dark brown, and frothed into lunatic boiling curls... I did all these hairstyles to look different, but underneath: same old face. Very rare canary legs and a sort of gossamer shift...those were the days. Shoes (model's own) still rather shabby.

Sometimes, however, the pictures took a more interesting turn. These, by Lidbrooke, were for an article about the psychology of sex in clothes. The PVC coat and star-studded sheer shift are a country mile away from cosy jerseys and tweed skirts. Lidbrooke took a morning to set up the shot, then only took seven or eight frames, very unusual in the age when 40 or 50 rolls per shot was commonplace. The photographer couldn't know for sure until the contact sheet came back from the darkroom whether or not the pictures were what he or she wanted. In the starry dress I think I look a bit like a centaur, half horse, half woman.

Looking glamorous meant no smiling and quite a lot of staring deep into the lens. The fake leopard coat was a favourite garment, worn with my mother's choker of paste diamonds. When it was stolen I was very set down. Black knee boots will never go out of fashion, only the heels and shapes of the toes change. My poppy-covered blouse had been made to order; my hair had just been cut short and I think I felt uneasy about its new length. Crimpers often cut hair too short because I think they get carried away by the sharpness of their scissors. My panama hat was a trade mark and for a short while I was the only holder of a British passport with the subject wearing a hat.

I collected old Victorian chemises and shirts: this strange picture shows a lovely Persian wall hanging and a doubtful woman in dodgy lighting.

Opposite, on holiday in Greece, in 1966, aged twenty, as ever practising to be better at my chosen career as somebody, anybody, in front of a camera.

Always present a moving target: don't get stuck with 'a look': keep changing and they won't find you out. I still have the blue and white Liberty Jean Muir dress with puffed sleeves, but the grey straw hat has gone with the wind. Lurex cut low, cowboy gear and lariat, Gypsy Rose Lee…there was nothing we wouldn't wear or do. Modelling stood me in good stead for my future career in the changeable profession of acting.

And Introducing...

In the old days, if, in your screen debut, you played an important part, it always said in the credits '...and introducing So-and-So as "Lorinda Gazebo"' or whatever the character was called. If the first role you played was not of a noteworthy size this didn't happen. As I had sloped in through the back door, as it were, was in fact blown up before the front credits rolled in my first film 'Some Girls Do', I was denied the peculiar thrill of being introduced to a grateful audience at the beginning of a dazzling career. I hadn't been to drama school, or been in repertory theatre; I had been a photographic model, which in those faraway times was considered the most pitiful and unhelpful background for an aspiring actress to have had. You had to belong to the actors' union, Equity, to work: and you couldn't get your Equity card unless you had spent 42 weeks in the theatre, or had played a speaking part in a film, but you couldn't be cast in a film because you didn't have a card... it was a Catch 22 conundrum. The change of direction from modelling to acting had been playing on my mind for some months. I had been in several television commercials and thought that I could use that brief experience to blag my way into the film world, but the Equity card, or lack of it, was the barrier. Then suddenly a knight in shining armour appeared in the handsome form of the great Shakespearean actor Richard Johnson. I met him at a party in Chelsea and told him how hard I was finding it to get over the threshold into the world of entertainment. He said 'I'm doing a film at the moment: I'll get you to be a small character with a line to say, and then you will be given an Equity card'. And that is exactly what happened. The film, 'Some Girls Do', was a Bulldog Drummond story and my part was a robot who fiddled about with wires and blew the building up at the command of some sinister officer played by James Villiers. My line was 'Yes, Mr Robinson' so perhaps he wasn't an officer, but I had my card! I was a professional actress!

'Let's start at the very beginning...' Looking as casual as a first-timer can , smokes on the ground, paint-stained, what-the-heck jeans, Pinewood Studios here I come. Only one line to say: and the door to the profession swings open.

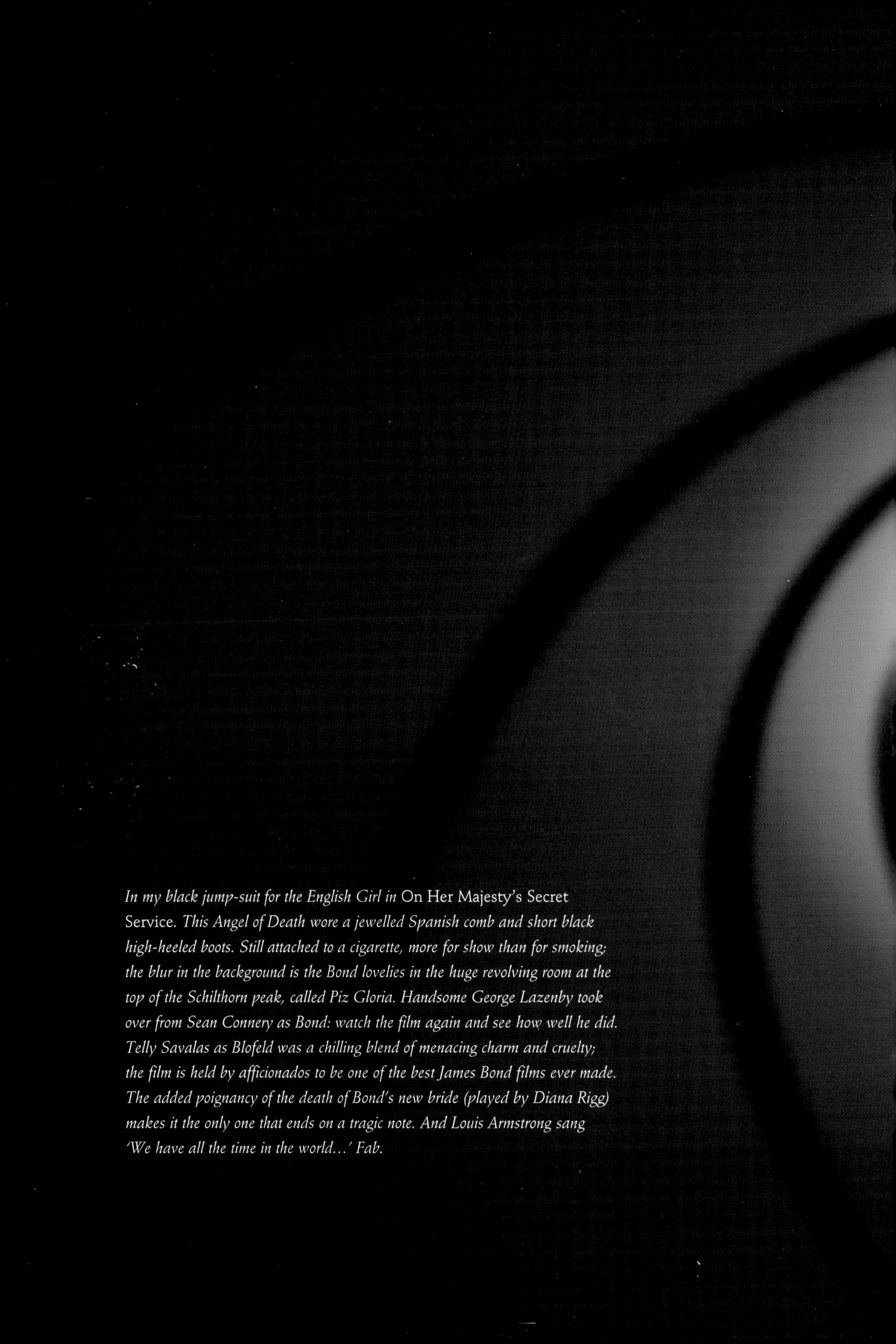

In my black jump-suit for the English Girl in On Her Majesty's Secret Service. *This Angel of Death wore a jewelled Spanish comb and short black high-heeled boots. Still attached to a cigarette, more for show than for smoking; the blur in the background is the Bond lovelies in the huge revolving room at the top of the Schilthorn peak, called Piz Gloria. Handsome George Lazenby took over from Sean Connery as Bond: watch the film again and see how well he did. Telly Savalas as Blofeld was a chilling blend of menacing charm and cruelty; the film is held by afficionados to be one of the best James Bond films ever made. The added poignancy of the death of Bond's new bride (played by Diana Rigg) makes it the only one that ends on a tragic note. And Louis Armstrong sang 'We have all the time in the world...' Fab.*

We often lined up to do publicity shots like these. Sometimes the same picture printed in black and white gave magazines the chance to make it look like a fresh shoot.

With the optimism of youth I imagined it would always be possible to work if you were punctual, talented and polite. To be cast as a Bond girl was a stroke of sheer good luck, as London was crammed with pretty would-be starlets and any one of hundreds of girls could have played an Angel Of Death in Blofeld's glamorous army of assassins trained in germ warfare. There were twelve of us; and in the superb story '*On Her Majesty's Secret Service*' we were garrisoned at Blofeld's secret hideaway in the Swiss Alps for two months. Autumn gave way to winter, and the Bernese Oberland changed from golden-orange to grey, black and white. Every day we were up before dawn to put on fairly extravagant costumes and make-up, and have our hair done: then we caught a cable car up to the summit of the Schilthorn, a cage full of twittering birds of paradise, supervised by a character called Irma Bunt, grim thuggish warden of Blofeld's experimental clinic. It was completely thrilling to be involved in such a colossal extravaganza. The village of Murren where we were based was sealed off from the outside world for six months, Bond's Aston Martin was airlifted in, stuntmen arrived by helicopter, the circus had come to town. (Forty years later, when I was travelling on a ferry in Sudan, my arms were grasped by an enthusiastic Arab who recognised me as a Bond girl, even though I had only spoken two or three lines in my part as the English Girl: so great was the impact of those films.)

The sensational Piz Gloria circled by the mountains of the Bernese Oberland. Even today it boasts of its proud links with James Bond.

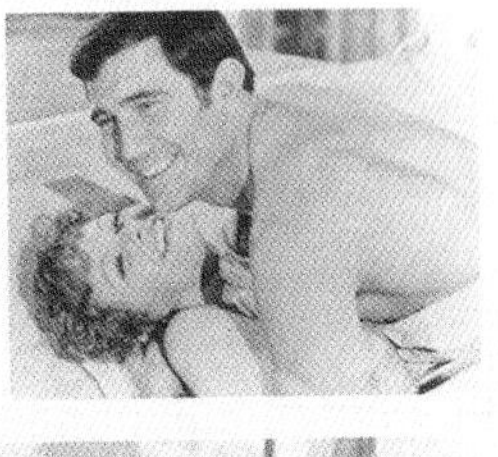

ON HER MAJESTY'S SECRET SERVICE
25th ANNIVERSARY SPECIAL

Blofeld's 'Angels of Death'
The Piz Gloria Girls

25th ANNIVERSARY SPECIAL
007 MAGAZINE
THE PUBLICATION OF THE JAMES BOND 007 FAN CLUB
ALBERT R. BROCCOLI and HARRY SALTZMAN
JAMES BOND 007
IAN FLEMING'S
"ON HER MAJESTY'S SECRET SERVICE"

1. "You are funny at pretending

...Hanley was first spotted in a cinema commercial by a talent scout for Harry Saltzman. She met with him and was offered a five-year contract, from which Saltzman was subsequently forced to release her. The contract didn't exactly ... a vast amount of work, ... her brief part in *OHMSS*, ... go Jenny unbelievably ... hat must be the worst ... of them all!" Curiously ... ere as the Italian girl, on ... credits of *OHMSS* she is ... girl. Her other films ... *of Dracula* (1970) with ... *Percy's Progress* (1974) ... Madeline Smith, and ... tles (1974). On TV in ... ound fame as co-host of ... *Magpie* and has also ... *rsuaders*. ... Dinah Sheridan and ... ley, her brother is ... irman of the

...dinavian girl

...ay, Jule Ege's ... oluminous to list here, ... *Home Should Have One* ... *World Forgot* (1971), ... *Deadly Sins* (1971) ... *Up Pompeii* (1971) ... nith, *Go For A Take* ... aska Hempel, *Percy's* ... Jenny Hanley and ... TV appearances ... in the comedy

... (Zara)

... determined

... (Mona Chong)

... includes brief ... olly (1969) and The ... 69) with Diana ... Curt Jurgens.

6. "Course I know what he's allergic to."
SUE-ANN, the English girl
(Joanna Lumley)
Clearly believing her role in *OHMSS* insignificant - she has described it as "only set dressing, like a vase of bright cushions" - Joanna Lumley has appeared in a handful of feature films. Among them are *Some Girls Do* (1968), *The Breaking of Bumbo* (1970), *Games that Lovers Play* (1972), *The Satanic Rites of Dracula* (1973). However, it is her consistent work in TV that has made her a household name. She has had starring roles in *Coronation Street* (1971), *The New Avengers* (1976-77), *Sapphire and Steel* (1979-80), and most recently *Absolutely Fabulous* (1992-93).
In 1989 Joanna read an abridged version of Ian Fleming's OHMSS over 10 nights for BBC Radio 4's series *A Book at Bedtime* and she is now featured on a new series of James Bond spoken word audio tapes. She has also featured in a plethora of lucrative television commercials, both in a voice-over and on-screen capacity and enjoyed much acclaim in a range of theatrical productions.

7. THE AUSTRALIAN GIRL
(Anouska Hempel)
Anouska Hempel's other films include The Scars of Dracula (1970) with Jenny Hanley, *Go For A Take* (1972) with Julie Ege, *Tiffany Jones* (1972) and *Double Exposure* (1976). Anouska, or Lady Weinberg as she is also now known, is a successful couturier and owner of the fashionable Blakes Hotel in London.

8. "Please, what is besant"
NANCY (Catherine Von Schell)
Nancy is, like Ruby, one of the more promiscuous among Blofeld's 'Angels of Death'. With the aid of a finger nail file she overrides the electronic locking system which confines all guests to their quarters, and slips along to Bond's room after dark. He finds her waiting for him on his return from his earlier clandestine meeting with Ruby. Despite our - and Bond's own - momentary concern that he may not be able to rise to the occasion, as we leave the couple, there seems to be little doubt that by morning Nancy will be nothing less than completely satisfied; she is, after all, in the hands of the indefatigable James Bond.
Catherine Von Schell (soon after *OHMSS* she changed her name to the less cumbersome Catherine Schell) was among the Piz Gloria girls given little more to do than simply look decorative. She has since appeared in many other films, including *Moon Zero Two* (1969), *Madame Sin* (1972), *Callan* (1974).
TV appearances more recently include *Clothes In The Wardrobe* (1992).

9. SYLVANNO, the Jamaican girl
(Sylvanna Henriques)
A former Miss Jamaica, Sylvanna also appeared in *The Lost Continent* (1968), during the shooting of which she was badly burned in an accident involving special effects explosives.

10. THE GERMAN GIRL (Ingrid Black)
Before appearing in *OHMSS*, German-born Ingrid appeared in three German-based film productions, though nothing is known of her work since.

11. DENISE, the Israeli girl
(Helena Ronee)
Another German-born actress, Helena also appeared in *The Adventurers* (1970) directed by Lewis Gilbert.

12. THE AMERICAN GIRL
(Dani Sheridan)
Born in Great Britain, Dani also appeared in the films *The Sorcerers* (1967) with Boris Karloff, and *The Brides of Fu Manchu* (1966).

...ces where The Piz Gloria girls are named, these are as they appear in the combined continuity version of the script. Names were probably only inserted to simplify identification, since in the actual film most remain anonymous.

0041

Andrew Sinclair's best selling first novel *The Breaking of Bumbo* was made into a film. Richard Warwick, who was unforgettable in Lindsay Anderson's 'If', was cast as Bumbo, a guard's officer who rebelled against the system, and I was his girlfriend Susie. I remember so well the feel of the gauzy see-through dress I wore in one of the scenes, scratchy and be-jewelled, with gem-encrusted pants, and the uneasy feeling of real wrong-doing when I assisted in the demolition of a waxwork of Winston Churchill. Very soon you learn as an actress that you will have to do and say things which are contrary to your beliefs; but you must become the advocate for the character and your job is to inhabit the person and present her as completely as possible. I hated taking my clothes off for bed scenes (I don't know a soul who is happy with their gear off in front of a large crowd of strangers or, worse, friends). We all had to do it, with varying degrees of success. If you had a 'phwoarrr' body, well and good: if you looked like me, polite clearing of throats. We filmed at EMI/MGM at Elstree which was under the control of Bryan Forbes. On the first day of shooting Forbesy gave me a book; he has never stopped reading and being brainy, quite apart from being a fine actor and director. Isn't it strange that actors are only meant to be interested in acting. As soon as you step outside the box and offer opinions on world affairs, literature, engineering, human rights, you are treated with incredulity, as though you have affronted the natural order of things. Jury members are picked at random, and their deliberations have far more serious consequences, but no-one would think of testing them to see if they were fit to pass judgement on the fate of a fellow human being.

The prickly but rather lovely dress with jewelled knickers. I clearly thought they were only going to use the top half of the photograph, hence sad leg-positioning.

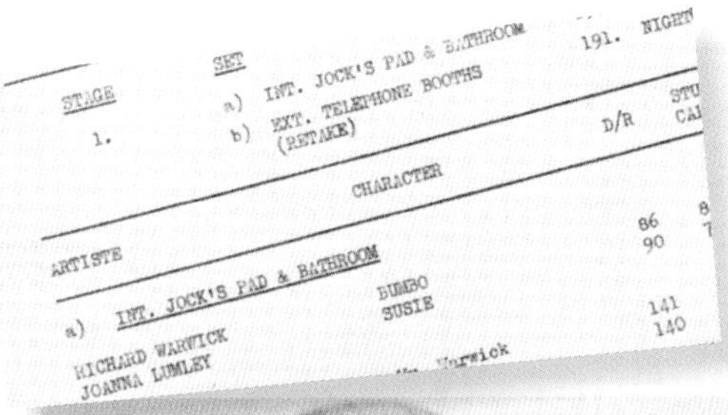

STAGE | SET | 191. NIGHT
1. | a) INT. JOCK'S PAD & BATHROOM
b) EXT. TELEPHONE BOOTHS (RETAKE) | D/R
CHARACTER
ARTISTE | 86 | 90
a) INT. JOCK'S PAD & BATHROOM
RICHARD WARWICK | BUMBO | 141
JOANNA LUMLEY | SUSIE | 140

Richard Warwick had the rare quality of being loved by everyone who met him, ancients and toddlers, men, women and animals. He laughed like a drain all the time. When we had to do a nude scene we were given a bottle of champagne to loosen us up: it just made us laugh even more.

THE BREAKING OF BUMBO
THE BREAKING OF BUMBO RICHARD WARWICK JOANNA LUMLEY NATASHA PYNE JEREMY CHILD JOHN BIRD DONALD PICKERING

Ava Gardner was in her early forties when she appeared in the film *Tam Lin*, directed by Roddy McDowall, in the year when man first landed on the moon. As a latter-day witch she moved amongst a clique of acolytes, fell in love with Ian McShane who in turn was enchanted by Stephanie Beecham playing the local minister's daughter. The film was never released, but it was given all the treatment a star vehicle should have. The costumes of her coven were custom-made; mine included dresses by Jean Muir and a sensational pink velvet coat by Rupert Lycett Green. The location was Traquair House in Peeblesshire, a small but historically important castle whose famous Bear Gates will never be opened again until a Scottish king is crowned in the British Isles.

Ava, 'Big A' as we called her, was glorious. Ravishingly beautiful, with a handspan waist, she was friendly and approachable; and when she heard I was throwing a party for the minor members of the cast she insisted on turning up at my second-floor rented flat in Addison Road, with her faithful manservant Reggie in attendance carrying a basket of whisky, gin, vodka, tequila, rum and brandy. These she tipped with abandon into a tall china jug and handed out to the guests; shortly after drinking the mixture we could scarcely remember our own names, and the party rocked on until dawn. I thought the world of her: on the first night of the shoot I picked some briar roses for her from the hedgerows and knocked timidly on her door. Her maid let me in and Big A asked me to read Ian McShane's part for the scene she was to shoot the next day. Soon she got tired of rehearsing and, calling for drink ('It tastes better from the bottle'), she asked that the swimming pool in the basement of the sombre Peebles Hydro Hotel be opened so that we could swim. She brought along her dog Cara and her maid Louise and we splashed to and fro as midnight struck. It was whispered that her ex-husband Frank Sinatra still telephoned her every day; theirs was a love that endured all kinds of challenges and rode through all the storms.

The Tam Lin *shoot was dream time: so much hanging around in the soft gardens of Traquair House, so many friends (Michael Billyard-Leake watches me playing 'Moon River' on a mouth organ) and a ravishing wardrobe by Jean Muir. The brown silk jersey and long wool spotted dress were some of many I wore, to be seen only as a glimpse in the background. I have kept all my Jean Muir dresses. They are timeless.*

So I was in films: but what about television? How could I get into that world? A television drama called *The Mark 2 Wife* nearly brought an early end to my short and scrappy acting career. I cannot remember being more afraid. My part was tiny, but to make it worse it came right at the end of the play, which was performed almost as if it were on stage, with takes lasting fourteen minutes. I had hardly been called to rehearse as my part was so pitifully small (but all important: I WAS the Mark 2 Wife), and as the moment came for me to swing open the front door and arrive during a monumental marital tiff, in a silver crochet dress with my heart beating louder than a ship's engine... well, I thought I might as well pack it in, as nothing could be worth such agonising torture. From that terrifying experience I have learnt something: be utterly prepared, and hang around watching everything everybody else is doing, and listen to what the actors are saying so that when your words come out you sound at least as though you are on the same planet. Fear has always been my greatest enemy. I know that if you can get that tyrant tamed you are due for a happy life. Easier said than done.

Was it necessary to sit on a roof in a pair of shorts? Yes, if you were publicizing a play in Canterbury; the size of the cathedral forced me up to the chimney-pots to be in the same shot. The hot pants, as they were called, were made by cutting the legs off a pair of men's trousers. Biba boots, in suede, £12 a pair. Even then that was cheap as chips.

So I was in television: but how now to get into the theatre? Having lived my adult life by bluffing or blagging my way into things (pretending I knew what 'blocking' meant, or what it was to 'hit your marks' or even what 'calling the half' and 'get an inky-dink and kill the brute' referred to) I trooped along to the audition for *Not Now Darling* to play a titchy part as a secretary who had two lines in the first scene and one in the last. I didn't know where the 'prompt corner' was, didn't even know what 'upstage' and 'downstage' meant, but you learn fast. Needs must when the devil drives. The play was in repertory at Canterbury: soon after that I trod the London boards at the Garrick Theatre in a Michael Pertwee farce, starring Brian Rix and Alfred Marks, called *Don't Just Lie There, Say Something*. The feeling of walking up the Charing Cross Road and into the stage door, saying hello to the stage doorman and opening your dressing room door with a key, putting your bag down amidst all the familiar make-up and good luck cards, starting to get ready, chit-chattering with fellow actors... I thought this is the business for me. The play was later made into a film with a slight recast; Leslie Phillips took over from Alfred, but the film's budget was lower than a basement window and I don't recall seeing it in any of the big cinemas. No matter: work was work and everything was grist to the mill.

DATE

Anyway, my life had changed forever and for the better by the arrival of my little son Jamie. His father, the photographer Michael Claydon, and I never married, but have remained in the closest contact all through Jamie's upbringing and will do always. To be responsible for the most treasured creature on earth is a privilege known to millions of parents the world over, but I guess each time a child is born a bit of extra magic comes your way. Jamie was born in 1967 and he gave a new and proper purpose to my life; from that day on, his welfare became my overriding concern, and work, how to keep the wolf from the door, would be the prime target on my safari.

Farces often include cupboards, plain clothes policemen and mistaken identity. Here Brian Rix, Leslie Phillips and I try to explain our dilemma to Peter Bland, thereby displaying all three elements.

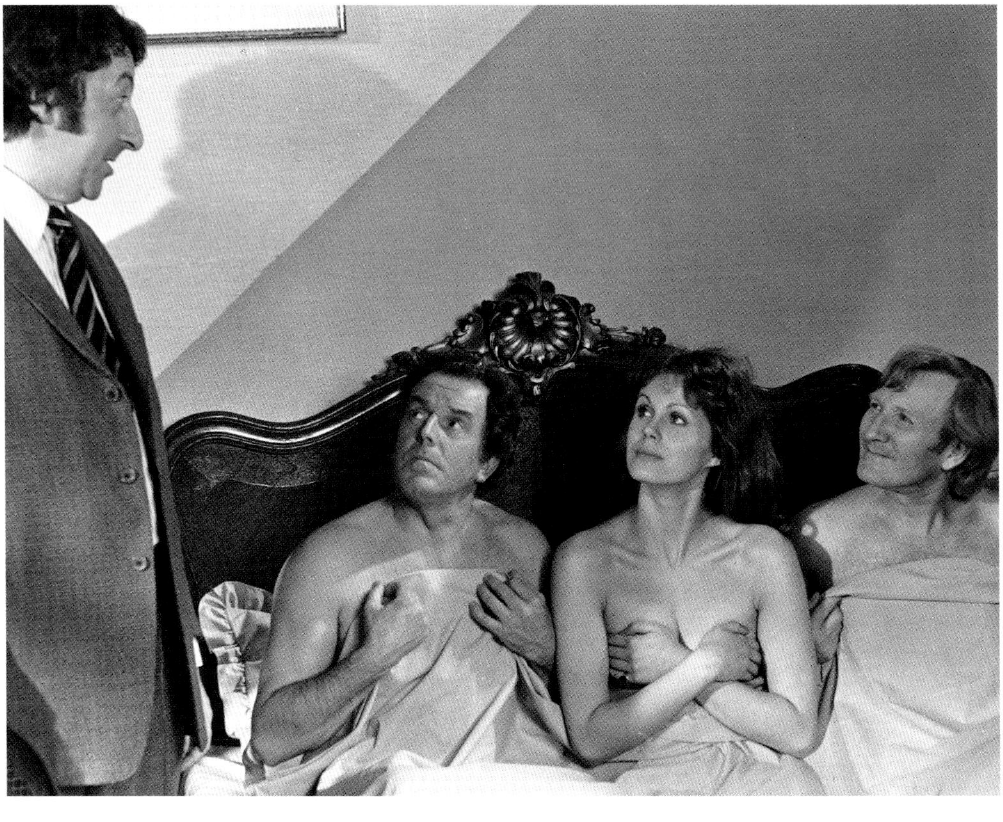

When you see pictures like this one of Leslie and me, it isn't us acting: it is us being directed from behind the camera. Below, however, we are reacting with horror to the arrival of the policeman. Or the politician's wife. Or a hippy with a spray can. I can't remember the details but the writer Michael Pertwee was at the top of his game.

Opposite: my beautiful 1949 Silver Wraith Rolls Royce, with Lucas headlamps and a kneeling Spirit of Ecstasy. She was maroon and black and as lovely as a mid-summer morn.

The sixties turned into the seventies. Regardless of the dull echo of an empty bank account I borrowed two hundred pounds from my reckless Aunt Joan Mary (she and my mother, when faced with a ludicrously inappropriate adventure, would always say 'Oh DO!') and added it to my last three hundred to buy a beautiful wreck of a Rolls Royce without ever having driven it. When I did, I found the immense vehicle had no working brakes. As soon as they were fixed I gave lifts to my impecunious friends and fellow actors to Pinewood Studios, or to Kent to stay with my long-suffering parents who loved the car and calmly put up with the stray people and dogs who were brought down to stay. Jilly Cooper, the hugely successful columnist turned novelist, wrote a sit-com called *It's Awfully Bad For Your Eyes Darling* which we recorded at the BBC. It starred (starred!!! we were stars!!!) Jane Carr, Elizabeth Knight, Jennifer Croxton and me. I invited Jane to stay during the six weeks we took to make the series, and she stayed for nine years and became one of my all-time best friends. I was still in the Brian Rix farce at the Garrick so every time our television show was aired the announcer was obliged to say 'Miss Lumley is appearing in...', a custom long-since dropped.

Elizabeth Knight, Jane Carr, Jennifer Croxton and me in the sitcom Jilly Cooper wrote. Jane had been Mary McGregor in The Prime of Miss Jean Brodie *and knew Maggie Smith, so she was halfway to the stars already.*

SEX

ROLLS
RR
ROYCE

Also in the show was Jeremy Lloyd, JL as I called him, a tall and dreadfully funny writer and actor; we had met on a grimly unamusing comedy film the year before, married within weeks and sadly divorced within a year. Maybe we just shouldn't have got married, me in Jamie's christening outfit and a funeral hat, at Chelsea Register Office with four guests on a sunny May day: but I don't regret it for a second and nor, I know, does Jeremy. We have stayed close as the days and decades race by, through remarriages and changes of address, through illness and success; we have somehow kept our vows in part without realising it. When we met we had two Rolls Royces and four hundred pounds between us and, as JL said, we could throw a saddle across the world and ride it through the universe (or words to that effect).

My hair was brown at this stage, dyed by me as ever, and frankly rather beastly. JL and I sit on his blue Rolls Royce: this makes us look like millionaires but we only had one rented flat and £400 in the bank.

Chelsea, May, sunshine, wedding. We both played fairly silly asses in It's Awfully Bad For Your Eyes, Darling. *JL went on to write* Are You Being Served *and* Allo Allo.

TUC 288

MCO 731P

Top: The Borsalino Rolls and my Mini outside the flat in Addison Road. Cold day: fake fur jacket and hat.

In the New Avengers, Gareth Hunt and I as Gambit and Purdey lean cheerfully on a wrecked car: we had probably just killed someone.

When I was very young I was given a garage, not a doll's house, and my passion was collecting Dinky cars. I loved the look of a car or a tractor, or in fact any wheeled vehicle including and especially my gipsy caravan and the golden coronation coach. My collection didn't survive the journey back from the Far East, as I probably gave them to a school friend, but the memory lingered on. As soon as I was seventeen I took my driving test and failed almost before I started for a) wearing a vast black hat that blocked my all-round vision and b) because I drove over a pavement. I continued to drive with L plates

TAXI

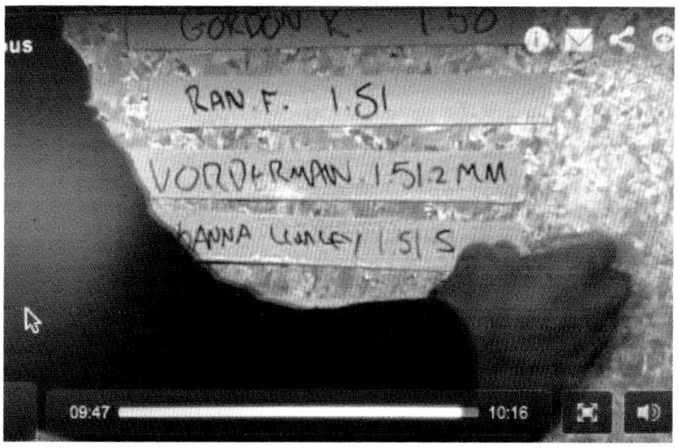
RAN F. 1.51
VORDERMAN 1.51.2 MM
09:47
10:16

for two years (often on my own: I was never stopped or reprimanded. We had a very louche regard for laws) and passed the test at my second attempt. By the time I bought the beautiful, brakeless, Silver Wraith Rolls Royce I had my second Mini as well; then I saw the film *Borsalino* and sent my Roller to be sprayed cream in the East End for about forty quid, a strange and reckless decision that lowered the already dismal value of the car to just above sea level. When I sold her, a dark day in my life, she fetched just £700. Three weeks later I heard she was being advertised for four times that amount. I've been lucky in my life with the cars I've driven, never luckier than when I appeared on *Top Gear*, tutored by the mysterious Stig, in the Reasonably Priced Car. I had to admit to Jeremy Clarkson that I had sold my red Ferrari (what type? – red) and now drove a Lexus and a Smart Car and he nearly fell off the platform with scorn. To drive faster than you normally dare, to hurtle into corners not believing you can pull the car through the turn, to accelerate when your body is shrieking to brake hard... this is petrol-head boy stuff, although many women have proved themselves not only equal to but faster than their male competitors.

And I still collect toy cars. In Africa they make them from discarded tin cans, very perfectly copied from life. I have a taxi and a Land Rover and a Smart Car too, and a big red American beauty which goes quickly on the floor when you vroom it up. A clown and a duck have joined in, both wind-ups; but I realise I have lost my golden coach forever and will have to wait until the next coronation to get another.

Deranged with fear I managed to become the fastest grandmother on Top Gear*, but brainy younger Vorderman still beat me. Being tutored by the Stig was a singular honour: he was very kind and patient and completely hidden by his helmet.*

12A
13
DD223

Why would anyone say no to being in a Dracula film, one that starred Peter Cushing as Professor Van Helsing and Christopher Lee as the fanged Count? I said yes at once: my part was Peter's granddaughter Jessica Van Helsing, and the film was released as *The Satanic Rites of Dracula* although we made it under the better title *Dracula is Dead... and Well and Living in London*. (Films often change their titles between shooting and release and quite often you miss seeing them altogether if your eye is not on the ball.) Left alone in a car with strict instructions to stay put Jessica creeps towards a ghastly house in a misty night. 'No Jessica!' you want to yell, 'Don't open that cobwebby creaking door into the cellar, you fool!!' But open it Jess did and saw to her dismay a friendly

PAN FILM
DD227
16A
17

DD230
19A
20

DD232
21A
22

KODAK SAFETY
DD367
4
4A

FILM
DD375
12
12A

FILM
DD378
12
12A

The only time I actually got to set foot in Coronation Street itself: my character Elaine Perkins was deemed too snooty to go to the Rover's Return so all my hopes of a career in Corrie were dashed to smithereens.

Coronation Street came at a time when I needed it most. I was very stretched for cash when I was asked to appear in eight episodes as the new and fleeting love interest in Ken Barlow's life, which had recently been shattered by his wife's electrocution involving a hairdryer. Maybe I would be so compelling that they would write me a permanent part and I could pop into the Rover's Return and get Ken his tea. But they had other better plans for the hero of the street and I was just a distraction for a mad month of his life. He asked me, Elaine Perkins, to marry him but being an idiot I turned him down (I had to; it was in the script) and a month later I was back in London with a clutch of letters I had written to every repertory company in the land asking for a job as an assistant or tea-maker or understudy. Only two replied: no room, not wanted.

I sit with a posh glass of sherry while Ken Barlow tries to excite me with the prospect of marriage.

Something would have to turn up soon, something quite wonderful. It's always darkest before the dawn: but those nights were very black and there was no moon. Just keep on keeping on: make lists and do small things, always look your best, pretend it's all such fun and moan with other actors about the state of the business when inside a little voice is saying 'Do you think you are cut out for this? Are you good enough? Why would anyone want you?' Accept everything that comes along, stay in the boat, try to reach the bank as the current drags you off course again... something will turn up soon.

And then something did.

In The End of Me Old Cigar *at Greenwich Theatre; I spoke only one line in the play, but had the unfading honour of working with Jill Bennett, Rachel Roberts and Keith Barron, and of meeting the great John Osborne who wrote the play which was a resounding flop. I am in the middle, next to Rachel, with nearly black hair and a tattoo on my arm.*

Opposite; having jumped from a blazing building, face attractively sooty, I broke my leg and a surgeon's heart in General Hospital *for six episodes.*

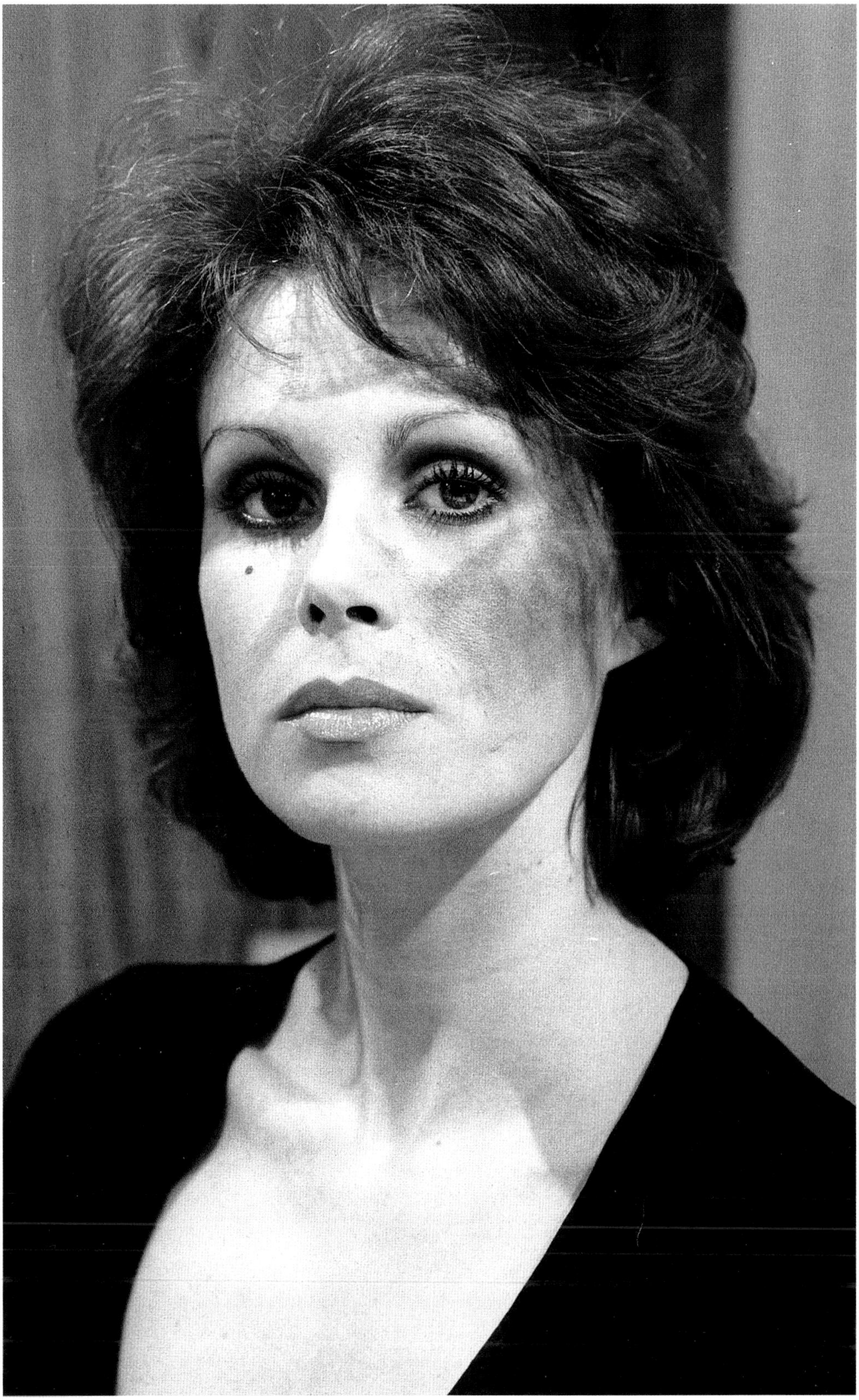

The Big Break

Opposite: in the second series of the New Avengers *my hair was longer: Albert Fennell, our producer, said mournfully that it was fatal to change hairstyles in the middle of a series but I was conscious of how many Purdey haircuts there were around, and wanted to ring the changes. These pictures were shot in France: Jillie Murphy was the stylist and wardrobe mistress.*

After it had been off air for ten years, it was decided to resurrect *The Avengers*, the massively popular adventure series which had teamed Honor Blackman with Patrick Macnee as partners in fighting crime. They had out-smarted super-sleuths, out-manoeuvred spy-busters and became general saviours of the world. Honor had been succeeded by Diana Rigg, whose universal appeal launched the show to the United States, and after her by Linda Thorson. The show pre-dated the Bond films by a year, and was the first to present a woman as equally tough and cool as a man. It was the most British of productions; Patrick Macnee, immaculate as the quintessential Englishman with a bowler hat and umbrella, was matched in elegance and wit by his leather-clad lady-friend. However, neither the BBC nor ITV wanted to back the revival, and so French money was sought.

The hunt was on for the new Avenger girl, and at the same time for a new male partner for Steed; it was felt that the action should be handled by a younger man, so that Macnee could remain aloof from physical skirmishes. Tremendous excitement and speculation followed the casting process: two or three hundred hopefuls went up for the new parts but no-one was chosen, although a shortlist began to emerge. After a tussle to get into the queue, I finally met the three producers, Albert Fennell, Brian Clemens, who wrote the shows, and Laurie Johnson, composer of the unforgettable theme music. They were singularly unimpressed by what I had done in my short and undistinguished career, and I had to beg them to give me a screen test to prove what I felt in my bones, that this part was mine, was meant for me. Times were as hard as granite as far as work was concerned: I had been lucky enough to get a modelling trip in Italy for a clothes catalogue, but the wolf was at the door and was waving his latch-key. Desperation made me bold: I MUST do a screen test for them, I would

ACTA
AGENCY COUNTERING THE AVENGERS
TOP SECRET
OFFICIAL DOSSIER ON
THE NEW AVENGERS
NOTES: This Dossier has A2 Security Rating and in case of enemy attack must be eaten rather than surrendered.

TOP SECRET

A file card taken from The New Avengers HQ.

CODE NAME: PURDEY

The New Avengers

Born Joanna Lumley

Date Undisclosed, India

Early Childhood Travelled in India, Hong Kong and Malaya with Gurka Major father.

Schooling International education including spell at Le Sorbonne, France.

Teens Ambition of becoming surgeon, horse rider, prime minister or ballerina (too tall).

Career Travelled widely (including Moscow) as successful fashion and photographic model. Acting.

Since Recruited by agent John Steed as second member of The New Avengers Team.

Description Height: 1,73 m Figure: 864-609-889 mm (34-24-35).

Drives MGB red white and blue.

Miscellaneous Deceptive, lithesome, eye-catching good looks, expert shot, deadly accurate high-jumping kick. Well versed in all forms of unarmed combat. Disguise a specialty. Fashion fiend.

show them that I was the girl they were looking for. Gareth Hunt, on the short list for the new male role, was to be teamed up with me; I flew back from Italy for a day at my own expense (ouch) to act out a scene with action and dialogue. It was a gruelling and exciting day; but as evening fell they said they would have to look at the work of all the other contenders before they could make any decisions. It felt bad: if they wanted me, wouldn't they say right now? The next day I flew back to Italy to continue the photographic shoot, my spirits at zero. I had hardly stumbled into my hotel room in Amalfi when the phone rang. 'Sit down', said my agent Denis Sellinger, 'You've got the part'. Can I describe what it was like to hear those words? It felt as though

Above: the leotard and tights are spot-on but a blazing disregard for Purdey's face and hair made this doll almost unsaleable.

Opposite: on Purdey's file card it shows her driving an MGB. in fact, I had a rather tricky yellow TR7 with no power steering: it was like a tank to park.

Incredibly flimsy dress, and high heeled shoes which had to be taped onto my feet if I was sprinting or shinning over walls. The heavy Purdey fringe annoyed our lighting cameraman because my eyes were often in shadow.

Video Gems
The Coach House
The Old Vicarage
10 Church Street
Rickmansworth
Tel: 0923 710599

The New Avengers

The black stockings (opposite) conceal my bruised shins, but although Gareth and I took a fair amount of battering during filming the fights and stunts we never broke limbs.

The day of our launch; as requested, the press photographed me in stolen stockings and suspenders, with a gun sensibly tucked into the stocking-top, which is one of an unmatched pair. Rolls Royce again, but this time with Steed's bowler and umbrella.

vast tectonic plates had suddenly slid sideways, as though I could hear the faraway screech and clang of their underground movement and I knew my life was going to change forever from that moment on. I waved farewell to the kind and generous modelling world for good, said goodbye to my familiar life of anonymity and stepped into a different way of being; a situation where I would be paid regularly, where I would work with the cream of British actors every day, where I would make the equivalent of thirteen feature films a year, and become as fit as a flea...where I would become 'famous'.

Gareth had been cast as Mike Gambit, and I was to be Charlie (or 'Charley'); I asked to change the name, as there was a fragrance on the market at the same time called Charlie and I thought we could do better, so I became Purdey, named after a model and the superb shotgun. It was essential that we were trained to be as fit as possible in a very short time, so Gareth and I were up before dawn every day to undertake a rigorous routine of shuttle runs, push-ups, sit-ups,

The New
Avengers

10 Church Street
Rickmansworth
Tel: 0923 710599
The New
Avengers

The New
Avengers

We did the publicity shots during our lunch hours when we were also interviewed for magazines, fitted for clothes and in my case taught to tap-dance (15 minutes allowed) and ride a motor bike (25 minutes and that's your lot). I funked the bike riding and got a stuntman in a wig to do it.

stretching and, in my case, sobbing for mercy. Gradually we became super-fit, limber and supple, fast and strong. There was much talk about Purdey's wardrobe: should she still be in leather, or in girly-gear, as we had two men already? Dresses and high-heels it was, and stockings and suspenders, which rather appalled me as I had hoped to present her as a tomboy. May I cut my shoulder length hair? Certainly not; whoever heard of a heroine with short hair. Oh please...and I did, and it was fine, more than fine, terrific (and tomboyish).

Before I had it cut (by an improbably handsome young hairdresser called John Frieda, assisted by a beautiful red-haired boy called Nicky Clarke) we had to announce the news to the press at an early morning photocall at the Dorchester Hotel in London. On the morning, just after 8 o'clock, dressed in my floaty clothes and a big smile, I was taken aback to find that unless I flashed my stocking tops the newspapers wouldn't print a single picture. But what were we going to do; I was wearing tights, and the shops weren't open. We walked into the Dorchester Hotel, found a middle-aged woman, frog-marched her to the Ladies' Room, tore off her stockings and suspenders, probably gave her a fiver for her trouble (and trauma), and then, dressed correctly for the press, I returned in the nick of time, with a revolver tucked into my stocking-top; the press sighed with relief. It was only after the event as I took the stockings off that I saw that they were not a pair.

Because Purdey had trained as a dancer her high kick was lethal, particularly to saps who dared to think that she was a bit girlie because of Flimsy Dress (see p119).

Pinewood Studios was the backdrop for many episodes, doubling as a stately home, a laboratory, a Ministry of Defence building and, in one episode, China. When the three Avengers drove together, Purdey always ended up in the cramped back seat, like a nodding dog in the rear window.

JUDO
柔道
柔道
JUDO

Fight days were my favourites: stunt men and women are my heroes in the industry because they are so incredibly disciplined, brave and accurate. Our action director Ray Austin, once a stuntman himself, taught me to run, kick, punch, fall, roll, climb, spin a car, fire a gun…and how not to moan even when things were grim. Over the page, Purdey protects an incriminating hand-print on the top of an old car. Going though the carwash, ordinary cold water jetting like cannons, being covered with buckets of detergent for comic effect on a freezing cold November day in Canada was something I will never forget. There was nowhere for me to rinse off the slimy suds: so the car wash was cleared and I stood in my underwear with power jets turned full on. Avengers never complain.

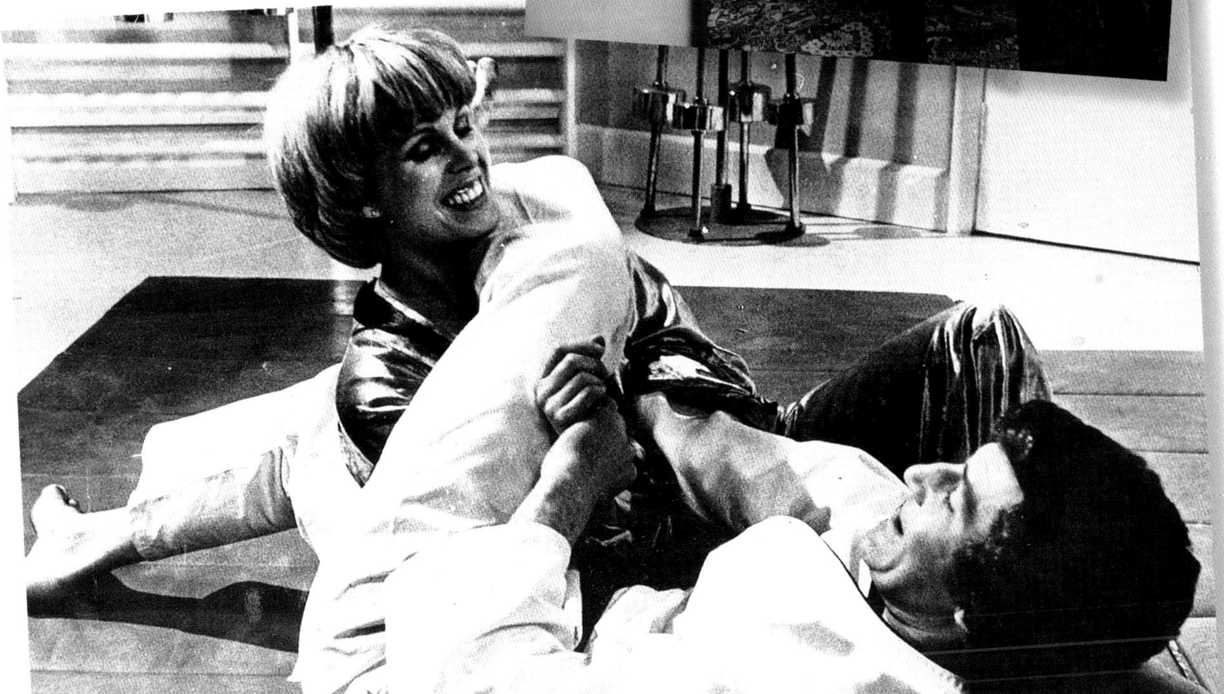

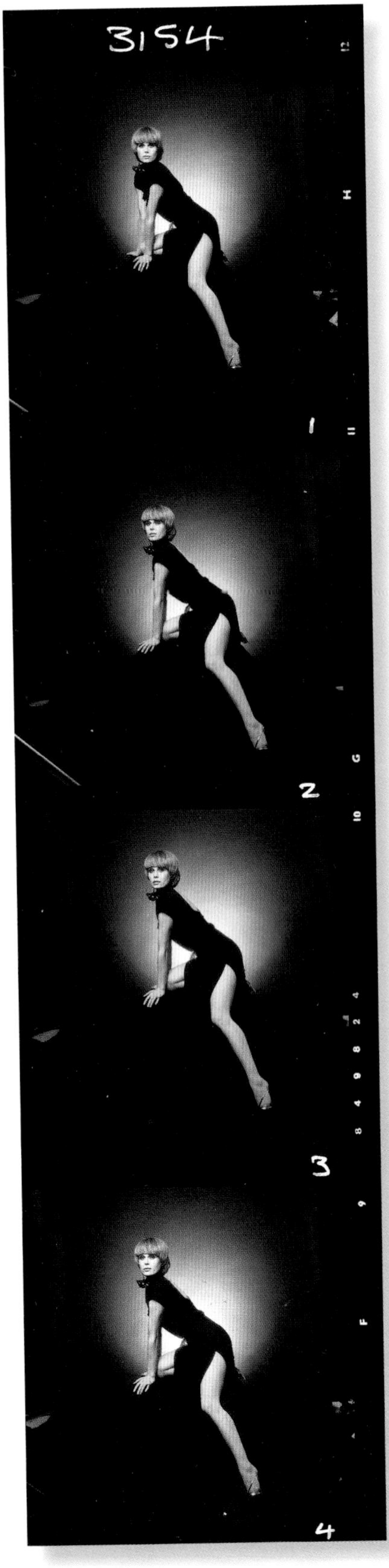
3154
1
2
3
4

I could not have loved my two years on the *New Avengers* more. Patrick, Gareth and I became firm friends for life: we worked so hard we were giddy and exhausted, but I got to do many of my own stunts and to work with the best of the best. The money was not terrific, and I didn't manage to struggle out of debt for years to come, but my undying gratitude to the producers and actors has never dimmed.

In the publicity we had to do, day after day, for publications around the world, I found that my real life had somehow been blended in with Purdey's rather racier background. (As a public figure, you have to get used to stories appearing which are complete fabrication and this was good training.) Suddenly I acquired a university education, at the Sorbonne, no less: and my father, in one version, had been a bishop who was shot as a spy. No matter; the pleasant lie that I grew too tall for the Royal Ballet has put me in good stead all my life. Each week the New Avengers saved the world as we overcame all obstacles, taking us to France and Canada, as the programme was re-financed further and further afield. The *New Avengers* had not only saved the world: they had saved me too.

Patrick Lichfield and Terry O'Neill took wonderful pictures of us all. The one on the far right is my favourite of Purdey: sensible jeans, but made a bit cheeky by not wearing anything under the flying jacket: hair not looking too pudding-y and a name on the helmet in case you forgot who she was. Stare down the barrel of the lens: that's the trick.

Bruce Oldfield made Sapphire's dress with light blue buttons on dark blue silk jersey.

David McCallum, the heart-throb Illya Kuryakin from *The Man from Uncle*, and I became *Sapphire and Steel* a year after the *New Avengers* had ridden into the sunset. As Sapphire, I could stop time with my alien skills and flashing blue-lensed eyes, and Steel, with his extra-terrestrial mega-brain, sorted out the evil that stalked our planet. For the next two years we worked in a dark studio with special effects and eerie, thrilling stories that scared our young audience. P. J. Hammond, the writer, had tapped into a vein of uneasy fiction where children vanished from photographs to re-appear in real life as grey wraiths, and a dead soldier of the Great War haunted a railway station where he had said his last goodbye before being killed. Some of the stories tested the notion of time past and present; with McCallum and our clever directors applying their incisive deductive powers we steered a path of logic through a complex web of intrigue. Sapphire wore blue clothes of strange and unfashionable design, because she was an alien and had no idea of, or interest in, the fashion of the day. She and Steel looked vaguely normal, although Steel was unable to behave like a human as he had no emotions and no empathy with the people he had come to

APPHIRE
STEEL

133
135
481

help. There was a children's television comic called *Look-In*: if you did look in, and thousands did, you would have seen us as a cartoon strip. It is very gratifying to be drawn as a cartoon character. I have kept a pile of the comics, and also an original front cover which depicts Mork and Mindy before Robin Williams became a movie star, Bob Geldof in his Boomtown Rats era, Christopher Reeve as Superman and us: a portrait of the favourite heroes of the time.

McCallum's dazzling good looks have never faded. My hair grew from shortish to long over the two years we shot the show.

The railway platform was so realistically made in the studio that people wrote in to say they knew the village where we had shot it. Sapphire became the schoolmistress the young soldier had longed to see again.

I was pleased to get my hands on a wig once in a while.

A Pink Panther location in the south of

Innocent Lies *started out with a different title. Oddly, I don't remember very much about this one except that it starred the excellent Adrian Dunbar, who had to carry me down a long flight of stairs, and that fine American actor, Stephen Dorff. He and Gabrielle Anwar played my children.*

Voicing animated films is an art of its own. You know what your character, or toy, looks like and how it will behave; you record the script like a radio play and the animators work to your sound track. Bob Hoskins was Teddy and I was the rag doll Annie (below right) in The Forgotten Toys; *the late great Clement Freud voiced a dog and the multi-talented Andrew Sachs did all the other voices.*

annie

-COLD-
COMFORT
-FARM-
-COLD-
COMFORT
-FARM-
January 1st 1995
at 9.30pm on BBC1
Starring
EILEEN ATKINS
KATE BECKINSALE
SHEILA BURRELL
STEPHEN FRY
FREDDIE JONES
JOANNA LUMLEY
IAN McKELLEN
MIRIAM MARGOLYES
RUFUS SEWELL
ANGELA THORNE
Directed by
JOHN SCHLESINGER
Adapted by
MALCOLM BRADBURY
From the novel by
STELLA GIBBONS
Produced by
ALISON GILBY
Photography
CHRIS SEAGER
Production Designer
MALCOLM THORNTON
Film Editor
MARK DAY
Music
ROBERT LOCKHART
Executive Producers
RICHARD BROKE (BBC Television)
ANTONY ROOT (Thames Television)
A BBC Television/Thames Television Production
BBC
THAMES TELEVISION

John Schlesinger directed the Stella Gibbons' classic Cold Comfort Farm *which had a raft of stars in it. Partly shot in London and then in Sussex meant that I only worked with Kate Beckinsale who played the lead, Flora, as my Mrs Smiling only featured in the London scenes. This often happens in filming; you pretend later that you rubbed shoulders with the whole team. And what a team this was.*

San Francisco was the location for the Roald Dahl movie James and the Giant Peach, *partly animated, and produced by Tim Burton and Walt Disney. Miriam Margolyes and I played Aunt Sponge and Aunt Spiker and had a bad time being winched up to be spun in a spider's web. Producer Jake Eberts didn't mind talking to me when I was in Aunt Spiker garb, with cunningly applied prosthetic make-up to make my lips thinner and my spiteful face crueller.*

Although it wasn't received with cries of joy, Prince Valiant *provided me with an enviable costume for Morgan Le Fay. The black leather dress and snake circlet were hot in the heat of a Berlin summer where we shot it; I had a stunt double, who was thrown into a cauldron of boiling stew.*

John Schlesinger directed Sweeney Todd *at the Ardmore Studios outside Dublin; Ben Kingsley played the Demon Barber, and as Mrs Lovett, gruesome maker of human pies, I was rigged up in blood-stained apron and a shrivelled wig with scabs in it. I asked John how he saw my part: he said 'I think she has bad teeth', so they were darkened down each day. This dark story was fun to shoot although Campbell Scott and I never got to hold hands as we do in this publicity picture.*

Mrs Lovett
Sweeney Todd

Albert Finney • Tom Courtenay • Joanna Lumley
A Rather
English Marriage
No Smoking
Marriage is a funny thing,
...isn't it?
BBC TWO

Once in a lifetime your prayers are answered : and when the go-ahead was finally given for the Angela Lambert story A Rather English Marriage *to be filmed I knew I had landed in paradise. Albert Finney and Tom Courtenay are simply the best: and more than that, they are the best company you could hope for. I cried when I saw the transmission; at the end the two frail old men danced slowly to 'I'm Going to Get You On a Slow Boat to China' and somehow their enduring friendship in real life blossomed out of the beautiful scene, so sensitively directed by Paul Seed. The clothes were from the eighties, so it was big shoulders and bling jewellery for my pushy, ambitious character.*

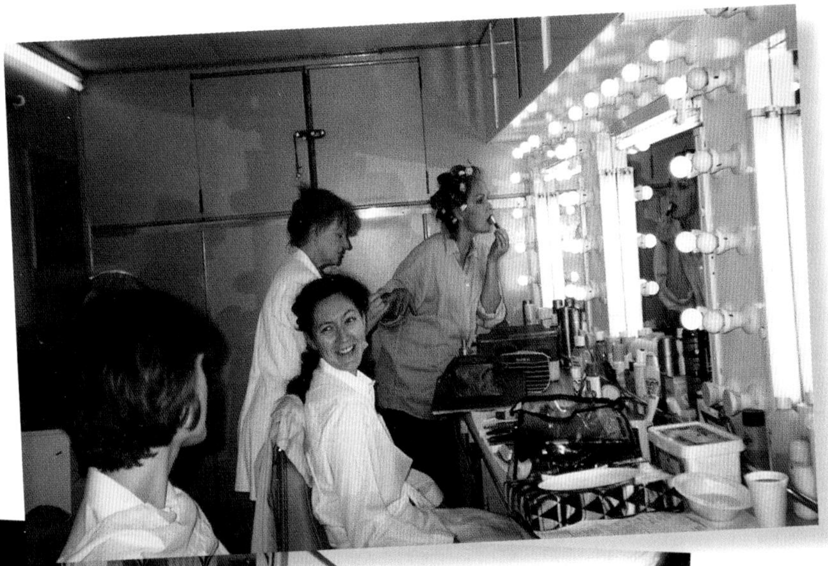

TOWN & COUNTY LIVING
ARTE BIANCA

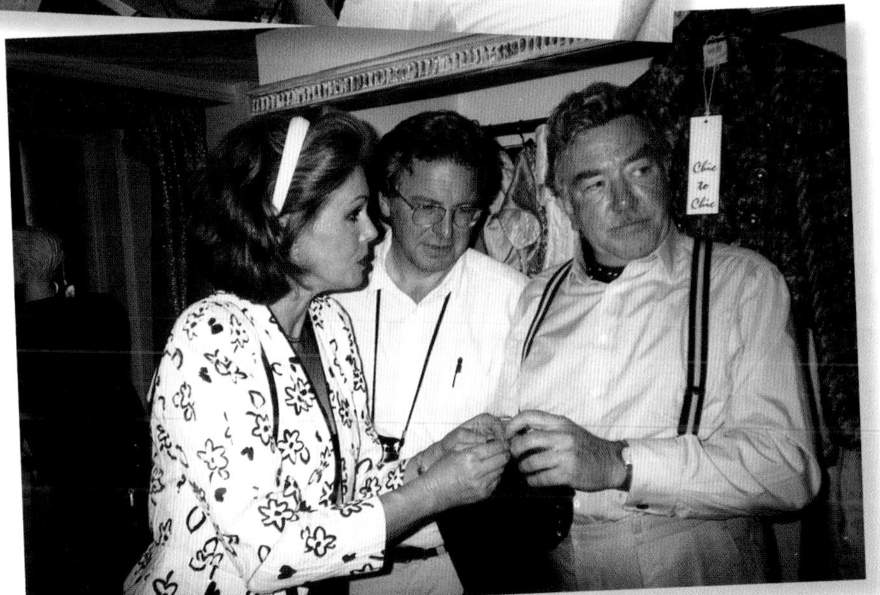
Chic to Chic

As you get older, so do your 'love interests'. Christian Kohlund and I nearly met decades before when he was squiring one of the Bond girls in Murren. We found plenty to talk about in our romantic scenes together as we sipped our ginger ale masquerading as champagne.

Given the whip hand (as I usually am) I can do my own make-up quickly and accurately. Elinor Glyn in The Cat's Meow *had dark red hair and marvellously kohl-rimmed eyes.*

Rachel stirling + Joely
MaybeBaby Richardson

Above: I spelt Rachael's name wrong on this polaroid, quite often the only record we have of the work we are in. Lovely to stand between the daughters of two glorious actresses, Diana Rigg and Vanessa Redgrave. The film Maybe Baby *was by Ben Elton and starred Joely and Hugh Laurie. (How were we to know he would become an American idol in* House. *Talented beyond belief. Nicer than pie.)*

Left: Tim Burton gave me this little figure of Maudeline Everglot, a character I voiced in Corpse Bride. *And no, I didn't get to meet Johnny Depp.*

Ermintrude, the opera-mad cow, in The Magic Roundabout. *Vain and yet endearing, I based her voice and attitude on Patricia Routledge as Hyacinth Bucket. Although the film starred Robbie Williams and Kylie Minogue I didn't meet them during the recording. Just as well, the way Ermintrude sang.*

La Bêt

Opening Night – October

VALERE
Well Heaven Bless Us! NOW I see:
It was a sudden burst of piety
That took you from the table, am I right?
I'm so relieved! I though, perhaps, your flight
Was caused by something I had said or done.
No, don't explain. GOD BLESS US EVERY ONE!
I, too, am very pious, most devout:
I cross myself ... twelve times (or thereabout)
Before I take my morning tea each day!
At lunch I'm up to forty; and I'd say
By night fall it's ... a staggering amount,
But what a foolish waste of time to count!
DEVOTION COMES TO NOTHING IF WE COME
TO SUMMARIZE DEVOTION IN A SUM.
A tiny play on words ... doth please you not?
I swear I made it up right on the spot!
I don't know how I do it, I just ... do.
These epigrams, they ... come to me as dew
Collects upon a budding daffodil ...
A curse? A blessing? Call it what you will,
It's mine to bear this "genius of the word"
DID I SAY "GENIUS"?; I think it's absurd
When people call you that, don't you agree?
To us it comes like breath: so naturally.
It seems like sorcery to those below!
I cite that telling phrase from Cicero:
"DE BONUM EST" ... "DIS BONUM EST" ... O, shit ...
Well, anyway, you get the gist of it.
I do love Latin. Does it show? It's true!
I'm something of a scholar in it, too.
I've read them all (yes, even I'm impressed)
From Cicero to ... you know ... all the rest
Whom I could quote in full without abatement:
But I digress ...

ELOMIRE
O, what an understatement.

VALERE
That meal! You must have gone to great expense!
How cruel of me to keep you in suspense!
DID I enjoy it? WAS the meal a hit?
I've turned you slowly, slowly on the spit.
Be at your ease, my friends! I thought the meal
Was excellent ... if not ... you know ... "ideal."
The vinaigrette: a touch acidic, no?
And I prefer less runny haricots;
More butter in the veloute next time;
And who, for heaven's sake, told you that lime
Could substitute for lemon in souffle ... ?
These tiny points aside, please let me pay
My compliments to all your company,
So generous in breaking bread with me
(Albeit bread that was a wee bit stale);
But I don't want to nitpick. Did I fail
To mention what a charming group they are?
Marquise-Therese! She's going to be a star!
A huge one! And it's not because she sings
Her talent is for ... Much bigger things.
As for the others, well they tend to be
A little too ... "theatrical" for me ...
But, darling, otherwise, words can't describe
My deep affection for your little tribe
With whom, I do amuse myself to think,
I shall be privileged to eat and drink
(As we have done this evening) every night!
That is, of course, assuming it's all right.
Am I mistaken? Stop me if I am.
But it seemed obvious to this old ham
That we had an immediate rapport!
Well-educated people I adore!
It's such a joy to know there's no confusion
When I, whose speech is peppered with allusion,
Refer to facts which few but scholars know:
Arcane, pedantic things like ... Cicero ...
And ... other larned oddments of that kind
(Which, to the truly cultivated mind,
Are common knowledge more than erudition ...)
But I digress! O, damn me to perdition!
"SHUT UP! SHUT UP! GIVE SOMEONE ELSE A CHANCE!"
I've had that said to me all over France
All over Europe, if the truth be told
To babble on completely uncontrolled
Is such a dreadful, dreadful, DREADFUL vice!
Me, I keep my sentences concise
And to the point ... (well, nine times out of ten)
Yes, humanly, I falter now and then
And when I do, naive enthusiasm
Incites a sort of logorrheic spasm.
A flood! I mean I don't come up for air!
And even though such episodes are rare
I babble on ... you can't imagine how ...
(My God! I'm almost doing it right now!)
NO; NO! I'M ONLY JOKING! NOT TO FEAR!
In fact, I'm far more guilty, so I hear,
Of smugly showing that "My lips are sealed ..."
When I'm the leading expert in the field!
Of haughtily refusing to debate
When I could easily pontificate!
Instead, I turn away with icy mien
And look ... intimidating serene
As if ... you know ... the wisdom of the ages
Were silently inscribed upon the pages
Of some majestic tablet in my mind.
But I lay claim to nothing of the kind!
It's others who surround me with this lore.
Myself, I know I'm just a troubadour
With very few accomplishments to boast ...
But, then, I'm more self-critical than most.
You think me too self-critical?! Alack,
Ten thousand more have launched the same attack!
That's awfully good: "... have launched the same attack!"
"Ten thousand more have launched the same attack!"
"YOU THINK ME TOO SELF-CRITICAL?! ALACK,
TEN THOUSAND MORE HAVE LAUNCHED THE SAME ATTACK!
That's VERY close to genius, don't you think?
If only ... YES! You HAVE a quill and ink!
I would be very grateful ... may I please?
No time to lose when lightning strikes the trees!
What did I say again? How did it go?
(Keep talking ... I'm listening, you know.
This won't take me a second.) Yes, that's right!
"Ten thousand more ... " O, what a pure delight!
One must act quickly on one's inspirations
That they're preserved for future generations.
Behaving otherwise, it seems to me,
Ignores the grave responsibility
Imposed on us (for it's not ours to choose)
By ... what? ... "the lyric gift" ... "the tragic muse" ...
I translate rudely from the words in Greek;
But any tongue sounds coarse when used to speak
Of something so ineffable and high.
Believe me, greater scriveners than I ...
(All right, not "greater", "different": is that fair?)
Have racked their brains and torn out all their hair
In vain pursuit of some linguistic sign
To name the art of uterus divine
But what? Poeticizing that's too crude
And I'm a stickler for exactitude
Who chafes at clumsy, earthbound turns of phrase.
True eloquence rings out like godly praise.
There's no mistaking it, it just takes wing.
And, frankly, my own word, "createring"
Seems loftiest ... more lofty than the Greek!
O! HOW DISGRACEFUL! SLAP ME ON THE CHEEK!
WHAT HUBRIS! WHAT VULGARITY! WHAT NERVE!
NO, SLAP ME! SLAP ME! THAT'S WHAT I DESERVE!
What gall that I, the commonest of sods,
Presume to speak more finely that the gods!
Of course it may be true, that's not the point!
What's ugly is my choosing to anoint
Myself instead of giving you the chance.
No doubt you both must look at me askance
For such a gross, conceited indiscretion:
I pray it won't affect your good impression.
I'm so relieved to get that off my chest!
Now that we've put that nagging point to rest
I shall return to my initial theme,
Which is, in short, in fact, to wit, I deem
By way if introduction, SILENCE ALL:
I HAVEN'T GOT A CLUE! BLANK AS A WALL!
NO, REALLY, I'M QUITE SENILE! IT'S NO JOKE!
MY HEAD IS LIKE AN EGG WITHOUT A YOLK!
AND DON'T THINK THIS IS JUST A WAY OF STALLING ...
MY MIND HAS BUCKLED ... ISN'T THAT APPALLING!?
THERE'S NOTHING BUT A SPACE BETWEEN MY EARS!
One time I had amnesia in Algiers,
Where everyone is black who isn't white!
(But that's another tale ... some other night.)
Suffice to say I lost a whole December ...
Or was it August? ... Whoops, I don't remember!
You see how absent-minded I can get!?
"WHEN DID YOU HAVE AMNESIA?" "I FORGET!"
Is that not comic genius? I must use it!
I'd better write it down before I lose it!
What did I say ... again ... about forgetting ... ?
O CHRIST! I've just FORGOTTEN! How UPSETTING!
COME BACK! COME BACK, YOU TANTALIZING GEM!
YOU TEASE! YOU BITCH! YOU FICKLE APOTHEGM!
I GAVE YOU LIFE, AND NOW YOU FLY FROM ME!!
This happens with annoying frequency
It leads me to exclaim and caterwaul!
Well! Now you've really seen me, warts and all
ALGERIAN AMNESIA! ... no, that's wrong.
O, never mind. More gems will come along;
They always do. Now where was I? ... Ah, yes.
You've seen me in a state of stark undress,
My warts exposed, my manner slightly odd.
Well, what would you prefer? Some cheap facade
Of blemishless perfection? Not from ME!
GO ELSEWHERE, YE WHO SEEK DISHONESTY;
MY LIFE IS TRUTH, AND TRUTH MY GREATEST PASSION!
Good heavens, both of you are looking ... ashen!
I've been too honest, haven't I? But when?
WHY CAN'T I LEARN RESTRAINT LIKE OTHER MEN
INSTEAD OF SPILLING EVEYTHING AT ONCE?
THE VINAIGRETTE! OF COURSE! I'M SUCH A DUNCE!
HOW COULD I? Please accept my deep regret!
Look, I ... enjoy ... acidic ... vinaigrette ...
It really makes me ... PUKE!!! ... O!!! THERE, YOU SEE!
I CANNOT LIE! DAMN MY INTEGRITY!
I want to spare your feelings, yes I do;
But that means saying things that aren't true,
And of my meager talents, that's not one.
You see, I find that dwelling in the sun
Of honest criticism brings more joy
Than rotting in the darkness of some coy
And sycophantic coterie of slaves.
God! Eloquence comes over me in waves!
Did you hear that one? We all raised our brows ...
Permit me ... just the ... finest of bows,
I thank you very much, you're far too kind;
As Cicero has famously opined,
"To hear one's peers applaud," ... no! That's not it!
You know the one ... the famous one ... O, shit!
THE ... ONE ABOUT ... THE NOBLEMEN ... COMPETING ...
Well, it's so famous it's not worth repeating.
The point is, when a man whom I revere
As highly as the famous ELOMIRE
Should greet my stabs at wit with such approval,
I faint ... go fetch a cart for my removal!
It's true. No, absolutely, I'm not acting:
The lights grow dim, my pupils are contracting,
My knees go wobbly and my knuckles white,
I'm fading out. Goodnight, sweet world, goodnight ...
I'm totally unconscious now, I swear.
CAN ANYBODY HEAR ME? ARE YOU THERE?
Perhaps you think I'm being too dramatic;
But, really, I just droop when I'm ecstatic.
What causes that? Do either of you know?
A mystic in Gibraltar said I'm low
In some peculiar energy which lies
(For Leos, Capricorns, and Geminis)
Astride the cusp of Saturn's largest moon.
Well, fine. But does that tell me why I swoon?
Of course it doesn't! What a lot of bunk!
Believe in that stuff and you're really sunk!
Thank God out age has banished superstitions!
(Except for things like sprites and premonitions
Which I think almost certainly are true;
And voodoo dolls and fetishism, too,
Seem eminently credible to me
And tarot cards and numerology
And cabalistic rituals and such ...)
But that astrology! Now there's a crutch
That's used by fools with half a brain, or none ...
WELL, SPEAK OF VISIONS! SOFT! I'M HAVING ONE!

10
anding in a public square in Ghent
it's Ghent. It look looks like Ghent.
ust say it's Ghent.") …It's Ghent.)
l banner reads: "A Great Event:
E VALERE and ELOMIRE Present
illiant Spectacle Hailed All Through France…"
en the title.) "ROMAN…," no, "ROMANCE
METHING…SOMETHING…" Then: "The Town of Ghent."
l you it was Ghent.) Then there's a tent
which throngs the very cream of Flanders!
g vision (though it almost panders
ising such glory to my dream
e two cloths sewn neatly at the seam
ents might, someday, this world enfold.)
, merely? Or a truth foretold?
omeone say which of the two he thinks it?
Don't answer: that would only jinx it.
e's a cranky governess gone gray.
d that phrase in Zürich, by the way.
was EIGHT YEARS OLD! YES, ONLY EIGHT!
ous? Try PHENOMENAL! Try GREAT!
y I provoked just knew not ends.
how despised I was by friends!
r fell in love with me of course;
ght my every word a tour-de-force!
him for doting on me so.
en, I was a…strapping lad, you know…
ok at me as if I led him on!
lame a child before you'd blame a don!!??
I ONLY DID WHAT I WAS TOLD TO DO!!
LIES! I NEVER JUMPED HIM! THAT'S NOT TRUE!
Good heavens! Suddenly it all came back!
So sorry… seems I wandered off the track…)
Um…FATE!…that's right…a governess gone gray.
She guides our every movement, and I'd say
Her stewardship goes well beyond the grave;
But if all things are fated, why be brave…?
Or noble? Or industrious? Or fair?
Is that all you can do? Just blankly stare?
Don't tell me this has never crossed your mind!
If not, you've waltzed through life completely blind!
Such questions are essential, don't you see?
A solid grounding in philosophy
Is vital to a proper education!
It never entered my imagination
That you could lack this bare necessity…
(The things I just assume! Well, foolish me!)
At risk of sounding pompous or uncouth,
I'd like to list some volumes from my youth
Which might flesh out the…bald spots in your learning.
They've made my brain more subtle and discerning,
Those great Moroccan-bound and gold-tooled classics,
Which we the prefects in our flowing cassocks
Had tucked beneath our arms…I smell them, still!
Indulge me for a moment, if you will.
I recommend you read…no, I insist…
An author whom, remarkably, you've missed
Since he's the cornerstone of ancient thought
(And if he's not already should be taught
To every child in every French lycée.)
His name, of course, is…wait, it starts with "A"…
A very famous name, don't help me out;
I know it's "A"; it's "A" without a doubt.
It starts with "A." It's "A." Or maybe "D."
No, "A." It's "A." I'm sure it's "A." Or "P."
I could be "P." Or "M." IT'S "M"! IT'S "M"!!
O, never mind. It could be all of them.
Well, this is terrible; I'm just appalled.
My God! He wrote the famous…WHAT'S-IT-CALLED…
COME ON! Don't leave me hanging on a limb!
You're acting like you've never heard of him,
And everybody has. He's world renowned!
His writings turned philosophy around
By altering the then-prevailing view
That what is real is really falsely true
To what is true is really falsely real…
Well, either way, it's BRILLIANT! Don't you feel?
And I'm not saying I don't see the holes;
Still, it's a stunning glimpse into our souls
No matter how you slice it, Q.I.D.
(He won a prize for it…deservedly.)
But who remembers prizes? It's the FAME!
The names of brilliant men like…what's-his-name…
Can never be forgotten: that's the PRIZE!
Such me live on when everybody dies!
They laugh at famine, pestilence and drought:
And isn't that what life is all about?
In any case, we've really talked a-streak!
Aren't you exhausted? Me? I'm feeling WEAK!!
We've hardly met, and yet you're like my brother
The way we banter and play off each other.
We've chatted, chortled, changed our points of view,
We've laughed a little, cried a little, too,
We've had some hills, some valleys and plateaus,
We've traded secrets, quipped in cryptic prose.
We've dropped our guards, we've learned to give a damn!
We've proudly cried, "Yes! This is who I am!"
We've said it all, and then…found more to say;
In short, we've, quote, "just talked the night away."
And surely that's a sign, at least to me,
That this our partnership was meant to be!
For though we're strangers (in a narrow sense),
In several ways more striking and intense
Our gift for words, our love of the sublime
We've known each other since the dawn of time!
O, very pretty: "…since the dawn of time!"
"WE'VE KNOWN EACH OTHER SINCE THE DAWN OF TIME!"
Well, good! That's all I really planned to say,
Except to thank you for a fine soiree
Spoiled only by acidic vinaigrette,
But then I've said that…more than once, I'll bet!
My head is in the clouds: pay no attention!
It's off in some ethereal dimension
Where worldly thoughts not instantly deleted
Are roundly and mechanically repeated
As if engaging the earth below.
How galling it must be for you to know
That even as we speak, within my mind
I might be off in some place more refined
That even though I'm present by convention,
You may not really have my full attention…
I don't mean you specifically, dear friend!
Good heavens! Would I dare to condescend
To someone as illustrious as you!?
I mean, of course, the common people who
Would stoop to kiss my hem they so adore me:
Forgive them, Lord! They know not how they bore me
With idle chatter of their simple ways!
I'm sorry, but my eyes begin to glaze
And it's a chore to keep myself from snoring
When someone's jawing on about their boring crop concerns
Oh no a blighted grape (my kids are all going to die)
I smile and nod, but silently escape
To knowledgeable regions in my dome
More crowded than a Roman hippodrome!
I have, for instance (and it's not a fluke)
Verbatim recall of the Pentateuch!
Incredible? It's true! Attend and see:
From Genesis to Deuteronomy
I now recite the Scriptures, LEARNED BY HEART!!:
"IN THE BEGINNING…"…yes, well that's the start;
It goes on just like that till Moses dies.
A superhuman task to memorize?
Not really. It's so good, it rather stuck…
But I digress! SHUT UP YOU STUPID CLUCK,
AND LET THESE GENTLE PEOPLE TALK A MITE!
Look, gag me with this handkerchief, all right?
I know that sounds extreme, and I'm a stranger,
But trust me: you are in the gravest danger!
For my digressions (left unchecked) can reach
The vast proportions of a major speech;
And you have no idea how close I am
To just that sort of frantic dithyramb!
So why not spare yourselves a living hell
And gag me! GAG ME! TIE ME UP, AS WELL!
RESTRAIN ME! DISCIPLINE ME! HOLD ME BACK!
HUMILIATE ME! GIVE THE WHIP A CRACK
DISGRACE ME: MAKE ME BARK AND WEAR A DRESS
AND LICK THE FILTHY FLOOR CLEAN UP THIS MESS
Rub my nostrils in your filthy socks
And if you have to lock me in this box
But in the meantime, gagged I should remain:
It's better that way, no? It's such a sane
And healthy way to curb my domination.
I find it a complete abomination
(No matter how distinguished one might be)
When every word is "ME ME ME ME ME."
ME, I'm far too interested in others;
And frankly, friends, were I to have my "druthers"
I'd utter not a peep for weeks untold,
Preferring to…absorb the manifold
Of human speech: the "babel" of the masses.
Just stop and listen to the lower classes!
You'll have an education when you're done
That rivals twenty years at the Sorbonne!
For in their mindless grunts, the bourgeoisie
Express what I call "wise stupidity."
But not one listens anymore, I fear,
And when I die, so too will disappear
That subtle art, whose practice now grows faint.
And I'm not saying I'm some stained-glass saint
Who always listens. Always? No, indeed!
My God! I'm human! Cut me and I bleed!
It's simply that, as far as mortals go,
I'm sensitive (and some say too much so)
To any nuance in a conversation
Which might, PERHAPS, suggest my domination.
Thus, in mid-sentence often I just cease…
(Despite the countless times I've held my peace
When, in the end, I might as well have chattered
Since only I said anything that mattered!
I know that sounds repulsive, but it's true.)
The point is, this is something that I do
Against all logic; so don't be distraught
If, in the middle of a brilliant thought,
I stop like this…depriving you of more;
Or if, commanding reverence from the floor
For awesome skills debating pro or con,
I simply stop like this…and don't go on!
A trifle strange, n'est-ce pas? But, if you please,
Ask any of my many devotees.
They'll tell you that this quirk (at first appearing)
In time becomes…incredibly endearing!
To me it seems obnoxious, heaven knows;
But most say it's a charming trait that grows
More sweet with each encounter! TELL ME WHY!
I just don't see it…but then who am I?
At any rate, THE GAG! OF COURSE! Let me
Observe with what profound simplicity
It does the job. I think you'll be surprised:
VOILA! Now isn't this more civilized!
I'm silenced and I think we're all relieved!
We've nipped me in the bud, and thus retrieved
The limelight for our precious Elomire.
Speak on, my friend! This player longs to hear
If in posterity you'll deign to share
Your splendid name with on AUGUSTE VALERE!
Please answer lest I talk you both to death.
I wait on your reply with bated breath.

Sometimes you are lucky enough to see genius at work in real life. Every time Mark Rylance soared through this colossal monologue you knew you were in the presence of someone truly great. During rehearsals I had to put hankies in my mouth to prevent myself from sobbing with laughter. Golden days: as gold as the fusillade of gold confetti that heralded the princess's entrance.

Being Fabulous

Right: Eddy and Patsy hit Paris. Pats believes she is looking fabulous.

Below: looking pretty fab before the day has really started; smoking de rigeur.

This is how it happened. Ruby Wax had come to see *Vanilla*, our doomed play on Shaftesbury Avenue, and she came backstage where we met for the first time. She said I should be working with Dawn French and Jennifer Saunders, but would I appear in her own show before that. I loved working with Ruby as she was completely anarchic, and preferred to improvise; and so we made up what we would do and say.

A few months later a script arrived out of the blue and I thought: I have never seen anything like this before, or laughed so much at a piece of writing. It was the pilot for a show to be called *Absolutely Fabulous* and Jennifer Saunders was the writer. I remember meeting her for the first time and she seemed intimidatingly opaque. I read through a scene with her and the producer Jon Plowman but I couldn't seem to make my character Patsy sound like the person she was hoping for. Jennifer can be very silent; on this occasion I felt so inadequate that I went back home, rang my agent and said: 'Get me out of this.'

'Oh come on,' she said, 'It's only a pilot, it may never get made, and anyway you are skint.'

All I can remember is inventing (for myself) a person, largely based on a cartoon version of me, who had her own life and history, and a way of walking with a hunched back, and a sneery voice, and trying it out in scenes with Jennifer. Once I got her to laugh I went on with more of the same. Patsy seemed to spring fully-formed into the world, with her heavy smoking and alley-cat morals, her sponging attitudes and foul language, and her undying jealousy of Saffy. Jennifer had opened a Pandora's box for me with her outrageously inventive writing. I don't know how or where she got her ideas from, but they were all new and fresh, shocking and desperately funny. She cast June Whitfield as her mother and Julia Sawalha as her daughter; Bubble

was originally to be a Sloane Ranger but as soon as Jennifer met Jane Horrocks she wanted Jane's accent.

With the confidence of genius, Jennifer would allow us to bring our own ideas about how our characters might develop; rehearsing for those shows was easily one of the happiest times of my life because we just laughed till we cried, day after day, suddenly sobering up for the live performances in front of an audience at BBC Television Centre. Every Friday, when the great theme tune 'Wheels on Fire', re-recorded by Ade Edmondson and Julie Driscoll, blared out into the darkened studio our hearts thudded and we would stare at each other, mouthing our lines or trying out a piece of business that had to work to get a laugh. It felt like a smash hit from the very first show: in the audience were not only Dawn French and Lenny Henry, but Ade, Ben Elton, Ruby Wax and a tooth-loosening bunch of top comedians which rather focussed the mind. But the applause and the gales of laughter told us all we needed to know: this one was going to run. But how far?

Jennifer often forges my signature and I hers: this is a rare item where we both appeared to have signed our own names. She can imitate my voice as well. We had both just finished a third margarita.

Of course we hoped it would be familiar to Londoners, and maybe the South-West of the country... but what about people who hadn't heard of Harvey Nicks and had no knowledge of the PR industry? The truth is that if a comedy is well written it doesn't matter where it is set or even who is in it. If it works, it works worldwide.

We filmed extracts in the South of France and Morocco, New York and Paris, always returning to record the complete show in front of a live audience; they can tell if something is funny, and we often had to hold up the filming until the hysteria subsided. It didn't seem to matter if we forgot lines, or if gags went wrong: the audience just howled for more. Edina's appalling taste in expensive clothes, and her exotic yet slutty lifestyle, struck a chord with them. For the first time on television a family was shown to be truly dysfunctional, with naked greed and bullying on show, and people laughed and called for more.

Patsy, who like me had been a model in the sixties, progressed from being a bitch to a witch, with many of her internal organs removed due to her catastrophic addictions to sex and drugs and rock'n'roll. Bubble was an airhead without any perceptible cognitive skills or abilities: Mother was light-fingered and blithely outspoken, Saffy was...well, Saffy was the only normal one in the show, a role which Julia mysteriously made completely unforgettable and sympathetic without a trace of goody-goodyness. Bob Spiers directed most of the early shows, and the comedy was served perfectly by his cool eye for humour and his ability to let the writing carry the show. We flew by Concorde to New York and back in a day, just to photograph a door-handle. We went on a photo-shoot to Morocco and Patsy sold Saffy in the souk. We rented a chateau in France but were too vain and silly

Cheers!
Joanna Lumley x

In Val D'Isere, where Patsy couldn't get off the ski lift and went round and round all night.

Outside the florist Moyses Stevens in Sloane Street: something about Eddy trying to find a suitable donation for the begging man and Patsy outraged that she is going to give away lovely miniatures of good spirits.

HNAYA

MOYSES STEVENS
£££'s

Patsy keeps her head on top of the 67th floor of a Manhattan skyscraper. Behind and below is Central Park. I have vertigo, and Jennifer, arriving by helicopter to rescue her friend from the tedium of office life, can't stand flying. All in all, a brave day.

Patsy
Fabfarely
38p
HADDOCK TIPS
Why Jo is Absolutely Lumley!
See Page 9
GLAMOROUS: Famous Lichfield pose
Jennifer has a mishap
WE STILL COLLECT GREEN SHIELD, CO-OP AND USED POSTAGE STAMPS
Purdey the ...
I'm no Patsy, insists Ab Fab Lumley
SEND NO MONEY NOW!
Lumley and Saunders
Joanna faces facts of knife
NEWS
Civil War President asks amazed doctors: 'Gentlemen, where am I?'
...t new drug brings back the dead
...BRAHAM ...INCOLN'S CORPSE REVIVED
...e's kept alive ...r 95 seconds!
EARLY DAYS:
TOP MODEL: A glittering
GLORIOUS: Joanna Lumley is clever AND funny
THAT'S SUN BODY!
Who is she? Pages 12 & 13
Sweetie,
MRS BOTTOMLEY: Her power is a turn-...
ABSOLUTELY ROMANTIC:
Hey Graham, have you seen who's looking Absolutely Fabulous on your beach..? See Pages 12&13
JOANNA LUMLEY: Lips are so tempting
CLEVER: Actre...
HADDOCK PERNODINE
HADDOCK STEW
NEWS
Screaming tourists flee when creature washes up on shore!
HALF-HUMAN HALF-FISH FOUND IN FLO...
Freak of nature stuns scientists
OLD BAGS...Edina has
We wanted Patsy to look absolutely gorgeous in everything she wears. Joanna is a perfect size 10 and has rarely
GREAT SHOW: The hilari...
...FUL: Joanna
Joanna still so sexy at 47

On the left a montage made by Jennifer for me, and below, one made by a fan.

ABSOLUTELY
FABULOUS
YOUR TRUE
ABSOLUTELY
FABULOUS

NEXT TRAIN
IS TO
TENTERD

is opening an ominously formal-looking envelope only to find inside a huge and unexpected repeat fee, for some show you had long since forgotten: lovely unexpected money.) So I say: 'Do unto others as you would have them do unto you'...it works.

And of course, there are all the people you would never even dream of meeting, from rock stars and heart surgeons, boxers and MPs, dancers and movie stars...to the Queen. When Her Majesty comes into a room there is an instant feeling of Something Huge About To Happen; will she stop and talk, or notice our group at all. Is it rude to stare very, very hard so you don't forget a single thing about that moment: will you remember every single syllable she utters, and try not to talk too much or too loudly or get onto some long-winded story you hope will amuse her...and then she is there! And words are exchanged and she is tiny and beautiful...and then she has moved on, and we all stand round grinning like fools. It is nearly the same thing with the Dalai Lama and Nelson Mandela: I have seen the same effect when Muhammed Ali was in London, and noticed people almost fainting as President Clinton passed by, but at the top of the list for me is the Queen. (I think – I know – Elvis would have fitted into this category too.)

The moment I love: "I now declare this arcade/building/ station/open!!!" and the snip of the scissors. I have cracked bottles of champagne which refused to smash and tried to cut tape with blunt blades; no-one seems to mind. Opening the Rolvenden Railway Station was a special honour as I had been brought up in the village.

The next two pages have a crowd of famous faces at events throughout the years. In the first spread you will be able to pick out Twiggy, Robbie Williams behaving badly, author Jilly Cooper, the heart surgeon Dr Christian Barnard, Gordon Jackson, Daley Thompson (what a schmoozy hug), Sefton, the horse that survived the Hyde Park bombings with his keeper, Michael Aspel during his (and my time) at Capital Radio (I was a director of the station for eleven years): you can spot Brian Cant, and playwright Harold Pinter during the run of Vanilla *which he directed, Gordon Brown when he was Chancellor of the Exchequer (we were to meet again years later, at Number 10 Downing Street rather than Number 11), a lamb, an elephant, and my lovely Shire horse Madame Butterfly, with me dressed up to give you a clue as to her name.*

Turn the page, and in no particular order appear Ken Bruce and Sue Cook when we were presenting BBC's Children in Need, *John Travolta at the* Baftas, *Greta Scacchi, Frank Bruno who hates being photographed, Professor Anthony Clare (I had just been on his radio show), Prince Charles at Clarence House (I am reading out citations for an award on the stairs), Virginia McKenna with balloons at the naming of an aircraft: there is Terry Wogan (with the present Mrs Wogan), Lionel Blair, Ernie Wise at a barbeque, Terry Waite at the opening of the Emmaus centre in South Norwood, the great Bill Travers of the Born Free Foundation, Julian Lloyd Webber (promoting real ale or the 'Quiet Pint' or 'Pipe Down', with all my support), Penelope Keith, Darcey Bussell, Patricia Hodge and Her Majesty the Queen at the Royal Academy; and for good measure, Her Majesty again, with Sylvia Sims in the background, at the Imperial War Museum.*

Mobil
30,000

Help Variety Club
build the new King's College
Children's Hospital
HiLo

DKNY JEAN

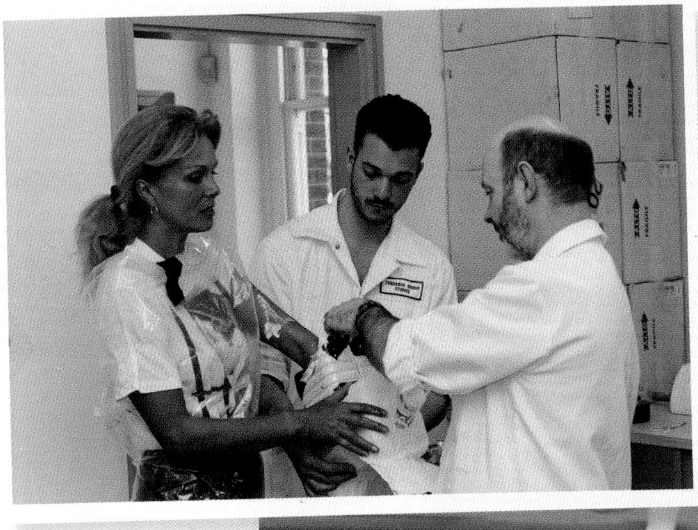

The plaster cast is taken off my arm. I'm still brown from my time as Girl Friday on her desert island.

Behind me are the photographs they took to ensure that every possible view of me would be accurate. Steve Swales works on the clay model of my head. I decided to smile, so that if people wanted to pose with the waxwork she would look cheerful: and they could slip their arm through hers and become my new best friend.

Many years ago, Adel Rootstein had my head modelled for the mannequins used in shop window displays; once I spotted ten such figures in the window of a New York department store, but even though I stood in front of them on the sidewalk for twenty minutes no-one noticed that they were meant to be me. To be made as a waxwork for Madame Tussaud's twenty years later was a tremendous honour. I was measured from top to toe, from side to side, from collar-bone to shin and elbow to hip. My hands were cast, while I stood stock still until the plaster had hardened, but the head, after being measured from nostril to lip and forehead to chin, was sculpted freehand by Steve Swales. Eyeballs were brought along to check the colour of the iris against mine: a tray of teeth, like ivory piano keys, offered a matching enamel colour. Luckily I had just returned from being cast away on a desert island where I had got a bit thinner (from lack of any decent food in the nine days I was there) so my figure looked less pudgy than it might have done. What would I like to wear? Jean Muir, I decided and so Miss Muir supplied her own choice, a navy blue wool jacket

We look like twins, but her hair is a bit bigger, and somehow her eyes seem bluer, an easy mistake to make, as mine change colour all the time, from grey to blue to green to sludge.

The near-to-nude shot, with the strange effect of skin-coloured hands contrasting with the grey clay of the model. Couldn't be happier. Or prouder.

and culottes, with solid silver buttons and a white silk jersey blouse.

The moment of unveiling seldom varies, apparently: it is always early in the morning, before Madame Tussaud's opens its doors to the public, so that there is a chance for the press photographs to make the next edition. Your model stands there, and you walk up to stand beside it: it is a strange emotion to be able to walk around yourself in real life, in 3D, as it were: is this how tall I am? Do I look like this from behind? My model has changed her clothes since Patsy came along: I think they felt that my clothes were too restrained, so a red dress was provided. The waxwork eventually moved from room to room, fitting into different scenarios, standing beside a piano or grinning with a group of comedians. Soon she will be gone, and her body will be melted down and her head removed to a shelf behind the scenes, where she will go on smiling, proud to be there, lucky to have been chosen, her long-lost hands for ever on her imaginary hips.

From Here to Kingdom Come

Opposite: Jamie in the green shirt was the youngest of the boys. Our journey into the high Karakorams was punctuated by dances, when the boys joined in, and mud-slides when we all got out to push the vehicles. Asif Khan gave me a Chinese road-worker's hat made of strong bamboo, rather than plastic or metal.

To Shimshal in the High Karakorams

I wasn't, but I feel as though I was born in a suitcase. Nothing sets the pulse racing as much as a map on the table and a case lying open on the floor; I love travelling, and feel it is in my bloodstream. The unknown attracts me like a magnet, and no matter how widely you travel the huge world is still rich in secrets and surprises. The chance to meet new people and eat different food, to find out about strange cultures and try to speak a difficult language...well, I cannot think of a greater thrill.

When Jamie was fourteen we were asked to join an expedition to a part of the world that my parents had known well: the North West Frontier, and the upper valleys of the Hunza region in Northern Pakistan. There were eleven of us, six young men who had just left school, Jamie and four adults. We set out to study the effects of the Ismaili religion on these remote regions, setting off from Rawalpindi and travelling through Abbottabad, where my sister had been born, to Gilgit and then on to Gulmit, a tiny village in the heart of the Karakoram mountain range. We travelled by jeep along the Karakoram Highway, sleeping in campsites, and leading a fairly rugged existence. There were landslips where the road disappeared altogether, and illnesses when everyone got sick from polluted water. The terrain was very rugged, scree and rock, with colossal gorges through which the grey Indus River rushed. Three of us, two boys and I, were joined by five Hunzakuts to make the arduous journey to Shimshal, a prison valley reached by a three-day journey through what seemed like the back of beyond. The scorching sun and strong winds, tiny stone huts and chilly glaciers made it wholly unforgettable. I wouldn't allow Jamie to come, as I didn't know for sure if we would make it there and back in safety. The bridges defied description, swinging perilously high above what looked like certain death. The village of

The rough path to Shimshal was exhausting. I got heat-stroke on the first day.

Joanna
Lumley

Try to imagine my fear at seeing this bridge for the first time. In the narrow gorges as we trudged eastwards towards Shimshal nothing moved but the wind, nothing sounded but the roar of the water below.

Shimshal was so hard to get to that it had been designated as a prison, as it was almost impossible to reach or escape from. Asif Khan, who led our expedition, was the younger brother of the great climber Shere Khan (like the tiger) who had accompanied Reinhold Messner on his mountaineering adventures.

The fellows from Hunza were tough and hugely good-humoured, moving like cats along paths that were only wide enough for a weasel. The tiny village, lying in a wide valley, had no roads as it had never seen a wheeled vehicle. The small dwellings had no chimneys, so smoke kippered you as you slept; but we were observed and welcomed with the greatest curiosity and kindness. The explorer Eric Shipton had written that the area was the most hostile he had ever crossed (which is quite something from the man who planned the successful ascent of Everest). No birds sang on the journey, and I only saw one flower in the seven days of our trek, a pale rose blooming by a boulder. In my daydreams I travel the route again; never before or since have I experienced such an extraordinary episode.

In Search of the White Rajahs

As a child in the Far East I had heard of the White Rajahs of Sarawak, an English family called Brooke, who had governed this small section of Borneo for a hundred years, running the tiny nation like a country estate. The film we made about their lives allowed us to travel as they would have done, paddling up rivers when there were no roads, sleeping in longhouses, trudging through jungles and trying to imagine how it was when head-hunters roamed the huge tracts of forest. The third and last Rajah, struggling to keep the country going after the Second World War, eventually sold Sarawak to the British government who in turn offered it to the newly-formed Federation of Malay States. The country changed hands for a million pounds.

Evidence still existed of the Rajahs' way of life; not grand but benevolent, with the Rajah making himself available to his people every evening at the Astana, the large bungalow that served as a 'palace'. I met and filmed his three daughters in America: they remembered rats in the roof, and no schooling, as they made their giddy way from Ascot to Sarawak's capital Kuching, from coming-out dances at the Ritz to the tropical downpours of an uncomfortable backwater jungle. Princess Gold, Princess Pearl and Princess Baba the press called them, although they weren't princesses; the middle sister, Elizabeth, married Harry Roy, the famous bandleader; he composed a song called 'Sarawakee' which was played in London nightclubs, while across the world the tribes of Sarawak, the Penan, Iban and Punan peoples had to get used to laying down their weapons against each other, as Rajah Brooke had outlawed head-hunting.

A safer bridge in Sarawak. The tropical climate brought back my upbringing in Malaya; hot and sweaty.

in SEARCH of the WHITE RAJAHS
A JOURNEY TO SARAWAK
WITH
JOANNA LUMLEY
BBC2
7.40 pm
Tuesday 24th September 1991
A WARNER SISTERS PRODUCTION

Learning to use a blow-pipe was easier than I thought; I would never have wanted to kill a bird or animal but target practice was fun.

CHARLES BROOKE G.C.M.G.

The few days I spent in a longhouse were salutary. Grannies stayed behind to look after all the babies, the young and strong went into the jungle to get food and medicine from the trees, pigs and chickens rootled under the wooden huts built on stilts above the forest floor. The children went to school by canoe and were lively bright little people, silent and respectful the second an adult shushed them, leaping in and out of the river like glossy minnows, owning nothing, expecting nothing and somehow having everything. The men had their bodies tattooed in the most intricate patterns: running through dense foliage they were as invisible as jaguars. Once we witnessed a funeral wake, with villagers from far and wide arriving with presents for the deceased to take on her final journey: and she was buried upright, ready to walk off into the next world when the weeping and wailing had ceased. But the logging conglomerates were already bulldozing their way into their tribal way of life: and now the majestic rainforests have been felled to make garden furniture and disposable chopsticks, and the tribespeople have been rounded up and put in camps.

Opposite: In a longhouse with the local chief, a charming courteous man who told me how much the tattoos hurt. He is dressed for dancing; the ancient costumes haven't changed through the ages.

The boat woman and I washing our hair in the clear jungle stream. The water was as warm as a bath.

Joanna Lumley ~ Girl Friday

Girl Friday on the Island of Tsaranbanjina

Would Patsy be able to exist on a desert island without a supply of drink and with Harvey Nicks out of reach? We thought instead it would be more interesting to see if I, Joanna, could survive with barest minimum of help on a tiny island called Tsarabanjina, off the north west coast of Madagascar, for nine days. I would be Girl Friday; trained for what seemed like only twenty seconds by the Irish Guards in Pirbright (above right), I set off on my trip, utterly unprepared for the hardships ahead. For a start, I had only some knives and sacking, a torch, and a rusty tin to cook in: I was given only three teabags and a pound of rice, the clothes I stood up in and the SAS survival booklet to show me how to make a bed out of sticks. I was allowed my drawing pad and a pen, and a flint stone to make a spark to light a fire, but no hairbrush or soap, no toothbrush, or camera, or books to read. I had a survival tin given to me by the dear Micks, the Irish Guards, which had three matches, some string and needle and thread, but no binoculars, no dish or spoon, no music...how was I going to manage?

Opposite above: with the Micks at Pirbright, trying to absorb instructions on how to build an earth oven. Below: my humble allowance of necessary kit for island existence is spread out on the sacking. I am inspecting my three tea bags and rice ration.

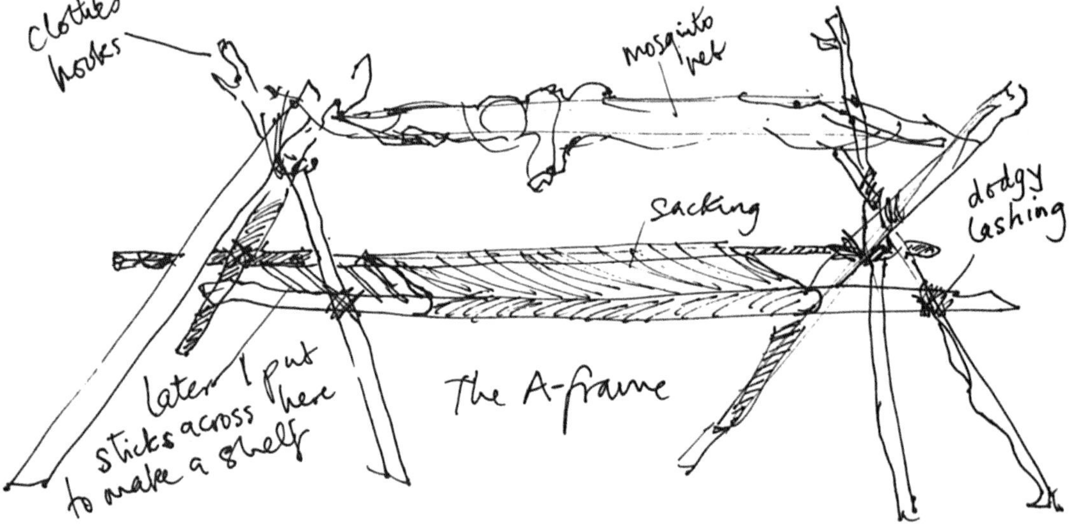
useful
clothes
hooks
mosquito
net
sacking
dodgy
lashing
later I put
sticks across here
to make a shelf
The A-frame

Making the A-frame bed. By drawing things you remember them more clearly. The tall poles had been left on the island by visiting fishermen but the place was deserted.

The small crew lived on a boat which was moored a mile out to sea: they came onto the island at first light, filmed all day and left before the sun set. A late monsoon meant that I had to live in a cave for four days, and when I returned to my bed, my A-frame bed that I had constructed laboriously on the beach when I arrived, it was full of twigs and insects. There was no fresh water supply, so I collected rainwater dripping off the rocks in a plastic bottle and purified it, which took ages. I found wood for the fire and spent hours carefully chopping the dry twigs into kindling and blowing on the embers to keep the flame alive for as long as it took to cook my grim supper each night, rusty rice with a fresh lime squeezed over to give it some taste, and eaten from a shell with a smaller shell serving as a spoon. The cave floor was sharp and rocky, cutting my bare feet, making my sodden-footed life miserable, so I cut up my cotton bra and stitched it to the insoles of my trainers to make the dearest little espadrilles.

The beach where I slept faced west. I watched the sunset, the flying foxes watched me.

The cave fire, with a tripod of twigs. The rusty can took ages to boil.

The cave fire

I watched turtle hatchlings trundling down to the waves: I was entertained by a school of dolphins who leapt and dived for quarter of an hour while I stood on the morning rocks above, shouting 'More! More!' My head was full of music I remembered: songs and tunes bubbled up, with poetry I had learned as a child: and, as hunger made me dimmer, I became obsessed with collecting shells spreading them out on the shelf of the A-frame bed. I propped one behind my candle stub to lighten the darkness of the cave. I named parts of the island so that I could remember where I was: Mosquito Alley, Skeleton Rock, The Albert Hall.

For nine brief days, nine days of eternity, I owned the island, watched over by flying foxes and fish eagles, surrounded by a crystal sea and the call of sea birds. I drew a map from what I could see, putting in all the coves and beaches. But I needn't have: it is securely sealed in my mind for ever, as fresh now as when I left by helicopter in the baking heat of my last afternoon, my footprints fading into the sand, a few shells scattered by the shore, leaving no trace but the A-frame and a buried offering of my rusty tin, a recipe for grubbed-up sweet potatoes and my SAS survival book.

My hair, caked with salt and sand, was in surprisingly good condition at the end of my stay. I always carried a knife in my belt, and never wore sunglasses because I wasn't allowed any.

Bhutan, Kingdom of The Thunder Dragon

In Bhutan, a country the size of Switzerland, there are only six hundred thousand people or so; Maybe and I could stare for miles without seeing any sign of human life.

Following in my grand-parents' footsteps, my cousin Maybe and I trekked across Bhutan in 1995, using maps, diaries and drawings of the country that had been all but closed to the outside world until 1930. In January of that year, my grandfather had been deputed to travel from Sikkim via Tibet into the landlocked Kingdom of the Thunder Dragon to confer upon the King of Bhutan the KCIE, the order of Knight Commander of the Indian Empire, as a mark of respect and friendship from the government of Great Britain. The King had asked that the ceremony should take place in Bumthang, a long march from the western pass over which my grandfather's retinue had crossed. It was mid-winter: they were met by bare-foot soldiers in splendid apparel, and they walked and rode for three weeks through the snowy mountains, resting at night in gorgeous silk-clad tents with braziers inside and orange trees in blossom outside, all prepared on orders from the King. With pack ponies and yaks, and carrying enough china and silver to throw banquets for their hosts, Grandpa Weir's expedition numbered about a hundred, with Granny's dogs coming

Joanna Lumley
in the KINGDOM of the
THUNDER DRAGON

Left: Grandpa Weir in the uniform of the Fifth Cavalry.

Below: The Weir contingent on their journey; they were greeted by splendidly-clad musicians and warriors with bare feet.

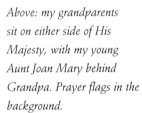

Above: my grandparents sit on either side of His Majesty, with my young Aunt Joan Mary behind Grandpa. Prayer flags in the background.

Left: after the ceremony the King and Queen of Bhutan posed for a formal photograph.

along for the ride; my seventeen–year-old aunt, Joan Mary travelled with them, equipped with her drawing things as she and Granny were accomplished artists. (My 10-year-old mother Beatrice was at school in England; she felt envious of this great adventure.) Unlike my grandparents, Maybe and I would make use of new roads and jeeps and waterproof tents for part of the journey: but we would have the luxury of sleeping in guesthouses and small hotels as well.

How much would the country have changed in sixty-five years? Well, there was an airport to start with, a small airstrip with a gaily painted building surrounded by mountains crowded in so close that you had to have special skills to land without smashing the wings of the aircraft against the steeply wooded hills. We went in October when the leaves were turning gold and smoke rose from village fires in slim straight plumes. Everywhere we heard the snap of prayer-flags, as this Buddhist country went about its daily round combining the tenets of the faith into all they did. The dzongs, monasteries crossed with administrative centres, hummed with deep-throated chanting, while the streets were buzzing with schoolchildren who had never seen television or played Gameboy. We camped in the high hills, and woke to find the tents and the porters' dogs white with frost; we washed our socks in streams and compared our trip with the notes and maps that my grandfather had made. When we arrived at our destination, it was resonant with ghosts of those long gone; afternoon sunlight slanted on to the floor of the shrine where the ceremony had taken place and dust mixed with smoke from butter lamps under the benevolent gaze of huge Buddhas half hidden in darkness. There had been an enormous feast prepared in the meadow outside the temple after the honour had been conferred, and all were invited, villagers and nobles alike. There had been archery and dancing: as we stood on the sunny grass we could almost hear the voices and the laughter, echoing down the years.

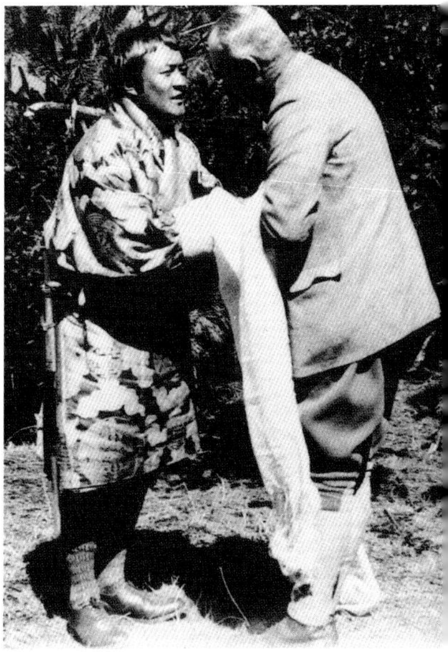

A touching farewell between two friends: Grandpa receives a ceremonial silk scarf from His Majesty.

When it was time for their departure, the King came with my grandparents to the wild hills, to the very border, to say farewell in person: he and my grandfather had become close friends in a short space of time. Presents were exchanged: on the list of British gifts, we noted that among the cloth and china was a trunk full of rifles. Bhutan still holds a strategically sensitive and important place between the great powers of China and India. She is still independent; long may she remain so.

Grandpa Weir could speak many languages fluently. While he was in Tibet, he studied Tibetan Buddhism and became something of an expert on the religion: much of his time was spent with the 13th Dalai Lama, as his duties and position put him in line to assist Tibet with the encroaching threat of a Chinese invasion. As spiritual and political head of Tibet, the Dalai Lama was an enormously important figure as well as being regarded as a god by his followers. A great and warm friendship sprang up between the two men and again many presents were exchanged. Our family homes are full of thangkas (religious wall hangings), teapots, statues and carvings from Tibet, Sikkim and Bhutan.

Our pack animals wind their way towards our next campsite. The high clean air and snow-capped mountains made our spirits soar. Sometimes we rode, but mostly walked.

The covered bridge at Paro hasn't changed from the time my grandparents crossed it.

Far up on the sheer rocky hillside hangs the Tiger's Nest monastery, Taktsang.

The Dalai Lama

When I had the invitation to go to Dharamsala to interview the 14th Dalai Lama about his forthcoming trip to Britain, my mother asked me to take one of the most treasured pieces in our collection: a wooden-ended book containing a scripture, a story of a saint, hand-written years before, and presented by the 13th Dalai Lama to Grandpa. In the Chinese invasion of Tibet in 1950, almost all the monasteries had been sacked and burned to the ground, with all their holy manuscripts

Meeting the Dalai Lama in Dharamsala, and giving him the scripture his predecessor had given to my grandfather. The wooden covers of the book were made in Nepal.

Opposite: a beautiful thangka of the Green Tara painted for me by Sarika Singh.

Indonesia and the Person in the Jungle

Anything that concerns the natural world concerns us all. If creatures become extinct because of man's behaviour I don't think we will be easily forgiven by the generations who come after us, let alone the creatures themselves. (Remember what that Greek philosopher said: 'If horses could draw, they would draw horses as gods'. We may yet have got it wrong.) It's not as if we don't know what's happening. The programme *Last Chance to Save...* invited me to Indonesia to see what was being done to try to save the Person of the Jungle , the orangutan, from certain oblivion. These tall distinguished apes lead a solitary existence, bearing one baby once every three or four years, hunting alone for fruit in the canopies of the rain forests, shy, powerful but no match for Man who is busy destroying every vestige of the habitat the apes need to survive. Loggers and the exploding population mean that there is an on-going struggle for territory, with the apes coming out as losers every time. The mothers are killed and the young apes are sold as pets. As they outgrow their cruel enclosures, some manacled to beds or hammered into crates, they become violent as a teenager would (and they grow at the same speed as humans; we are so like them it makes you gasp).

Jamie took this picture of the great red ape and me: orang-utans share many characteristics with humans, one of them being the ability to sit quietly in the grass thinking of not very much.

Primatologist Biruté Galdikas lived with the orangutans for years. She adopted the most vulnerable babies, who have to be taught to climb and eat and find food, just as our children have to be taught. There is a programme to re-habilitate the animals when they are able to fend for themselves, but thick and fast arrive more babies, wide-eyed and traumatised, clinging to any kind arms, helpless and stunned by their mother's death. The orangutans I met were fascinating; I was led into the jungle by one young ape with a baby of her own to look for her naughty little son, who wouldn't come when she called and when he did got a clout to discipline him. I watched an ape pretending to hammer nails into a plank of wood, carefully taking imaginary tacks from his pursed lips, watching slyly for our approval. We took three apes to be released and were greeted by the frankly terrifying sight of the wild orangutans swinging out of the jungle to meet the newcomers. (I saw an angry ape push a tree down with a sharp shove; you don't mess with these chaps.) The thought of a world without these giants is intolerable, and yet the clock is ticking, ticking, and the huge trees of the last rainforests on earth are crashing down as I write. What are we going to do? And more importantly, when are we going to do it?

Opposite: the silk curtain of the Aurora Borealis, indescribably thrilling to see with your own eyes.

Nothing: then... something! A green billowing in the sky, a flurry of what looked like harp strings, a soft explosion of crimson, like a firework in slow motion and the show began.

I'm not sure how long it lasted: two, three hours? I seemed not to be cold any more, wanted to lie on my back to stare at the whole sky, as the lights flicked and blazed across the inky blackness and the moon and stars could be seen shining serenely behind it all. I remember trying to stand still in the fierce wind so that the camera could catch me and the Aurora together; but their light is so strange that normal film cameras can't catch their colour, so you have to shoot at 10 frames a second, and then dilute the colour later because it becomes saturated... I know nothing of the mechanics of how we captured them: I only know we did, and for a moment I felt, for the first time in my life, as if I was in the universe itself and that all will be well. Whatever happens after this, I thought, all will be well.

Trying to stand without moving in a strong wind to be filmed with the Tricky Lady. We had ice boots and survival suits or I wouldn't be writing this.

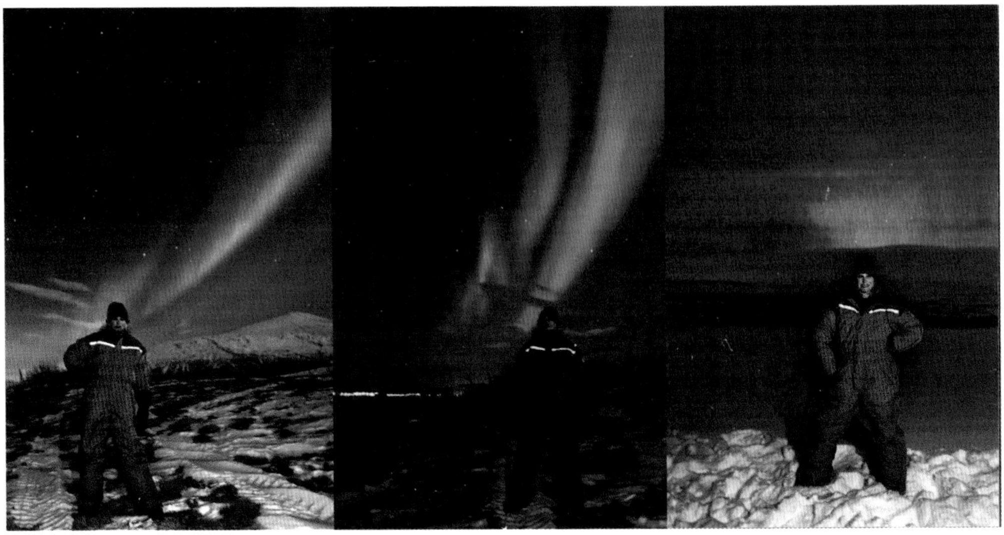

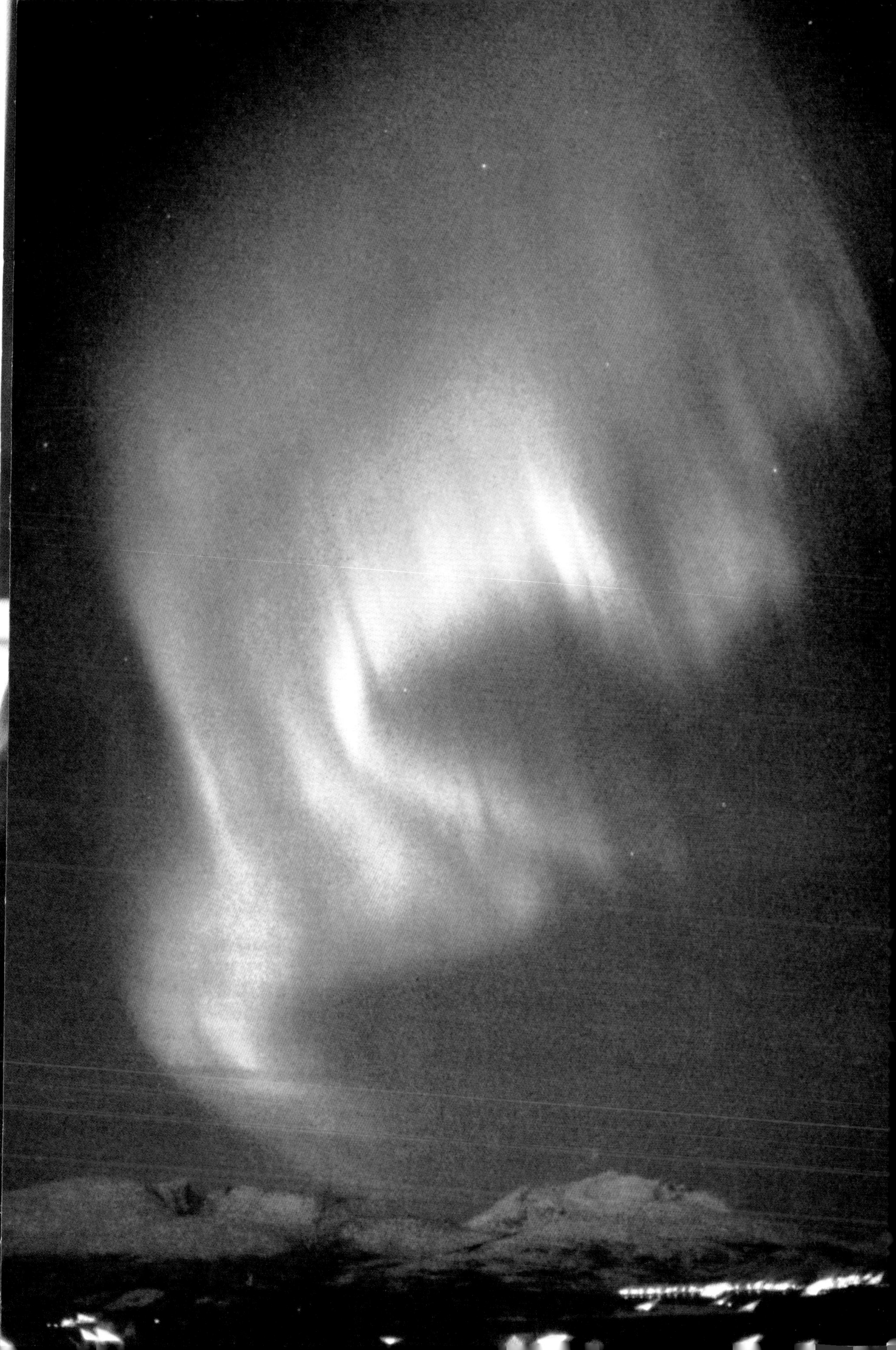

Above right: I carry this polaroid picture of Stevie with me wherever I go. I wish I could sing well; we look as though we have been trying out some Noel Coward songs at the piano in Wimbledon.

Right: what would it be like, I wonder, to read a music score like a book and hear every note of the whole orchestra? Stephen knows, and thinks it's completely normal. I am in awe.

I first nearly met Stephen Barlow when he was thirteen and due to come out to lunch with the son of friends of mine. (I was 21, and had already had Jamie.) The boy Barlow, by all accounts staggeringly musical and rather tricky, never arrived and I can remember thinking: 'Bother: I would have liked to meet that black-haired difficult boy.' Ten years passed, and my friends' son got married; and playing the organ at his wedding was black-haired, difficult Stephen Barlow. (When I set eyes on him I felt as though I had been given an electric shock.) We talked, exchanged addresses, nothing more as we were both tied up with other people. Eight years after that meeting I had a message out of the blue: he was rehearsing nearby, could he drop in for tea. And so our life together began, completely unplanned and unexpected, and continues to this day; soon we will have been married for twenty-five years. Do I believe in love at first sight, in fate, in luck? I do, I absolutely do.

We have lived in Wimbledon, where we ran out of money trying to buy a house beyond our means, in Kent in a marvellous and rather rickety parsonage, and in London where we hear Big Ben striking the hour and foxes yowling in the night. We bought a tumbledown ruin of a cottage in Scotland and restored it, bringing in spring water from the hills and planting trees where there had been none. Owls and bats and

PLEASE
DISCRI
GUR

Opposite: After the photograph appeared of me brandishing an unsheathed kukri, the famous curved Gurkha knife, an indignant man wrote to complain that I was carrying a dangerous weapon and should be prosecuted. The police used to say that you didn't need any security whatsoever during our rallies, as they were full of the most effective soldiers on earth.

education and to serve the Queen in whatever way they could…that was their aim. They didn't want charity: they wanted justice.

Peter Carroll and the law firm, Howe and Co, had submitted six test cases to the High Court of five Gurkha veterans and a Gurkha widow. Was it fair that men who had been prepared to die for our country were not allowed to live here? Would I help to publicise the cause? Could we get the British public behind us? Then started one of the most extraordinary and challenging campaigns imaginable. I can only write the barest bones of the proceedings: how we met, in cafes and doorways to discuss strategies, often emailing each other in the early hours of the morning; how all of us, engaged full-time in our 'day jobs', decided that, come hell or high water, we would never give in until we got the fair deal we were seeking; that Gurkhas should be treated like their Commonwealth counterparts. Martin Howe, David Enright and Kieran O'Rourke, the three lawyers who had prepared the case for the High Court, were indefatigable. Without Legal Aid no Gurkha would have been able to approach a lawyer; Legal Aid was vital, for without representation there can be no justice. More often than not it was just us five at the forefront, Peter, Martin, David, Kieran and me, attending enquiries, writing letters, rallying the

A GREEN VIEW by Iain Green
THE NEW GURKHA AVENGER
NOW I'VE GOT YOUR ATTENTION

mac
TRIUMPH FOR THE GURKHAS

From a huge fan. Best wishes — Mac

Daily Mail, Thursday, May 21, 2009

'Bad news, Sarah. Joanna Lumley has called a snap election.'

JOANNA GETS AN AB FAB RESULT

Joanna Lumley has won her campaign to secure settlement rights for Gurkhas. The actress, 63, whose father served with the feared soldiers, met PM Gordon Brown in Downing Street this morning ahead of the official announcement by Home Secretary Jacqui Smith.

BROWN U-TURN: P4

Mr Brown took all the cartoons in good humour; when he took up the reins from the Home Office, things moved at breakneck speed.

Overleaf: The press and media support was invaluable: by keeping our cause in high profile they put relentless pressure on the Government.

harder for Gurkha veterans to attain the stated criteria; Nick Clegg and David Cameron led the revolt, which received warm support from all sides of the House, especially from the back benches of the Labour party.

The end came on a sunny day, a day that could have been written by Enid Blyton. After more meetings and messages, chaotic interviews and speculation I was summoned to 10 Downing Street on May 23rd to meet the Prime Minister at breakfast time. Mr Brown's handshake was warm; I mustn't tell the press waiting outside what the decision was, he said, but I should be allowed to smile broadly. Massed in Parliament Square were the Gurkhas and well-wishers, with the police showing their support for the event by smiling from ear to ear; and stacked in front of them were the crowded cameras of the press and media. A transistor relayed to the hushed crowd what the Home Secretary was saying in Parliament: the Gurkhas would be allowed to stay! A yell, a roar went up, taxis hooted, bus passengers craned to see, cameras flashed, everybody hugged everybody else and we just stared into each others' faces and eyes...we had won. That afternoon the Prime Minister invited forty Gurkhas to have tea at Downing Street; and when a hundred and fifty appeared, the Downing Street police just waved them in with a grin. There were three cheers for the Prime Minister, cakes and biscuits were handed round, kisses flew and cameras clicked, and the bells of Westminster Abbey suddenly rang out; it may have been a practice session but I think it was the angels overhead, signalling that justice had been done.

With the red powder of a tikka, the Hindu mark of respect, covering my forehead, and great crimson garlands of flowers draped round my shoulders I make slow and happy progress through crowds of Nepali well-wishers. Looking up, I saw Jamie with his camera.

There are wrinkles to be ironed out as more Gurkhas apply to settle here, in small numbers, it is true, but they are arriving in a country already beset with its own financial difficulties: Dhan Gurung, the first Gurkha to be elected a councillor in the UK, has set up the Gurkha Services Link, and the service charities, especially the Gurkha Welfare Trust, continue with their unfailing support and advice. When you are building a new house you have to pause from time to time to see that you are doing it right, that the roof won't fall in, that the windows can open and close. Our country is historically reliant on immigration, and by welcoming the brave men of Nepal who have made it their life's duty to protect us, we are doing the right thing.

Our thrilling tour of Nepal later that year, the splendid receptions we were given everywhere we went, the love and gratitude that poured towards us, and towards the people of Great Britain, has made this one of the proudest episodes of my life. It was life-altering: a helter-skelter of learning curves, a tribute to the power of justice and the sheer goodness of ordinary people, an astonishing David and Goliath story with a happy ending, in the knowledge that a great wrong had been righted.

Would I do it all again? Absolutely.

AFP

For all the people with whom I have ever worked, everywhere in the world, with love and gratitude.

Photo Credits

The publishers would like to thank the following sources for their kind permission to reproduce the photographs and illustrations in this book. Every effort has been made to contact copyright holders, but we would be happy to correct any errors or omissions in future editions (Author's Collection except where stated).

John Adriaan: 74 (above right); 75 (middle row middle). 84 (right); 85. David Appleby: 134; 137 (all); 138-9. Brian Aris: 75 (below left); 152; 153. Clive Arrowsmith: 50 (above). Michael Barrett: 57. BBC Photo Library: 5; 74 (below middle); 105 (below); 190 (above); 191; 230 (above). BBC Top Gear: 107 (above left and right). Neil Campbell-Sharp: 255. Michael Claydon: 83 (all); 249 (below right). Wubbo de Jong: 253. Duffy: 66 (right). Freemantle Media: 4. Getty Images: 8 (above); 76 (above left, above right and below right); 104; 234; 235 (above left and below); 261. Annette Green: 94-5. Dinah Hasler: 250 (below); John Haynes: 141; 146 (all); 147. ITV/Rex Features: 169 (all). Wolfgang Jankhe: 158 (below). Jean Kertesz: 82. Giles Keyte/Baby Cow Productions: 190 (below); Mike Lawn: 163. Lidbrooke: 78 (all); 79. Lichfield Archive: 69 (above left, middle below); 74 (below left); 75 (above middle, middle left); 128 (left and right); 249 (below left). Jamie Lumley: 239; 257 (above); 271. Tessa Lumley: 251 (all). David Magnus/Rex Features: 92. Sylvia McMillan: 43; 45 (above and below). Richard Mildenhall: 143 (below right). Ed Miller/Baby Cow Productions: 190 (above). David Montgomery: 64; 65 (below). Terry O'Neill: 129. Sam Peek: 249 (above). Brian J Ritchie/Baby Cow Productions: 191; 191. Howard Rogerson: 74 (below right). Tony Russell: 162 (inset). Jennifer Saunders: 194(all); 195 (right); 196. Julius Silver: 90 (below). Peter Smith: 80. Sally Soames: 198 (all). David Steen: 81 (above). Peter Tauber: 113 (below); 124 (above). Martha Wailes: 216; 218 (all); 219. Crispian Woodgate: 52; 53 (all).

First published in Great Britain in 2011
by Weidenfeld & Nicolson

10 9 8 7 6 5 4 3 2

Text © Joanna Lumley 2011
Design and layout © Weidenfeld & Nicolson 2011

All rights reserved. No part of this publication may be reproduced, stored in a retrieval system, or transmitted, in any form or by any means, electronic, mechanical, photocopying, recording or otherwise, without the prior permission of both the copyright owner and the above publisher.

The right of Joanna Lumley to be identified as the author of this work has been asserted in accordance with the Copyright, Designs and Patents Act 1988.

A CIP catalogue record for this book is available from the British Library.

ISBN: 978 0 297 86499 8

Design by carrstudio.co.uk
Special photography by Martin Norris – www.martin-norris.co.uk
Origination by Alta Image, London
Printed and bound in Italy by Printer Trento and L.E.G.O. Vicenza

Weidenfeld & Nicolson
The Orion Publishing Group Ltd
Orion House
5 Upper St Martin's Lane
London WC2H 9EA

An Hachette UK Company

FSC www.fsc.org MIX Paper from responsible sources FSC® C015829

Endpapers: detail of a blanket from the Swat Valley in Northern Pakistan; Granny Weir bought a large number of these in the 1930s and they now adorn the houses of her grateful grandchildren.